the
KOAN
method

Copyright © Jennifer Lyn Simpson. All rights reserved.

No part of this publication shall be reproduced, transmitted, or sold in whole or in part in any form without prior written consent of the author, except as provided by the United States of America copyright law. Any unauthorized usage of the text without express written permission of the publisher is a violation of the author's copyright and is illegal and punishable by law. All trademarks and registered trademarks appearing in this guide are the property of their respective owners.

For permission requests, write to the publisher, addressed "Attention: Permissions Coordinator," at the address below.

Publish Your Purpose
141 Weston Street, #155
Hartford, CT, 06141

The opinions expressed by the Author are not necessarily those held by Publish Your Purpose.

Ordering Information: Quantity sales and special discounts are available on quantity purchases by corporations, associations, and others. For details, contact the publisher at hello@publishyourpurpose.com.

Edited by: Malka Wickramatilake, Tamera Bryant, and Lily Capstick
Cover design by: Nick Delgado
Typeset by: Nelly Murariu

Printed in the United States of America.
ISBN: 979-8-88797-060-8 (hardcover)
ISBN: 979-8-88797-059-2 (paperback)
ISBN: 979-8-88797-061-5 (ebook)

Library of Congress Control Number: 2023907392
First edition, September 2023.

The information contained within this book is strictly for informational purposes. The material may include information, products, or services by third parties. As such, the Author and Publisher do not assume responsibility or liability for any third-party material or opinions. The publisher is not responsible for websites (or their content) that are not owned by the publisher. Readers are advised to do their own due diligence when it comes to making decisions.

Publish Your Purpose is a hybrid publisher of non-fiction books. Our mission is to elevate the voices often excluded from traditional publishing. We intentionally seek out authors and storytellers with diverse backgrounds, life experiences, and unique perspectives to publish books that will make an impact in the world. Do you have a book idea you would like us to consider publishing? Please visit PublishYourPurpose.com for more information.

Jennifer Lyn Simpson, PhD

the
KOAN
method

Breakthrough Leadership
for a Divided World

Contents

THE FIRST STEP — 11

LEADING, NOW — 17

Chapter One—A World Divided — 21
Begin the Journey — 26
   HIKE Mantra — 36

Chapter Two—Alone in the Desert — 41
   Poetic Pause—A Stirring — 51

Chapter Three—Why the KOAN method? — 55
A KOAN Case Study: Embracing Innovation — 61
A Turning Point — 64
   Poetic Pause—Now, Empty Your Cup — 69

A DIFFERENT WAY — 71

the koan method — 79

Chapter Four—Cultivating Kind Cultures — 81
Creating Psychological Safety — 86
   CARE Mantra — 92
Beyond Bullying — 96
   Poetic Pause—Fantastic Things — 101
A KOAN Case Study: Radical Generosity in Action — 104
Empathy Heals — 108
Transforming Communities and Systems — 111
   HEAL Mantra — 118

Chapter Five—Fostering Open Systems	**123**
Building a Strong Foundation	128
TRUST Mantra	132
Systems Built on Secrets	136
Poetic Pause—Conversational Cartography	141
A KOAN Case Study: Open IDEO	147
Open = Receptive	150
Setting Inspired Direction	153
VIA(BLE) Mantra	162
Chapter Six—Being Adaptive	**167**
Being in the Now	171
BREATH Mantra	180
The Power of Presence	183
Poetic Pause—Zen Baby	187
A KOAN Case Study: The Million Dollar Conversation	191
Agile Evolution	195
Stay Relevant by Evolving	198
(VIA)BLE Mantra	204
Chapter Seven—Nurture Networks of Relationship	**209**
The Way Forward	215
JEDI Mantra	220
Connecting Across Differences	223
Poetic Pause—The Tao of Dickinson	227
A KOAN Case Study: It's Not Too Late (Networks to the Rescue)	231
Nurturing Networks: Building for the Future, Now	234
SUCCEED Mantra	240

BUILDING A COMMON GOOD — 245

Chapter Eight—The Future is Already Here — 251

Chapter Nine—In it Together — 257
   Poetic Pause—Universe at the Wheel — 267

Chapter Ten—Leading the Way — 269
   A KOAN Case Study: Leading into the Future — 273
     KOAN Mantra — 278

KOAN MANTRAS — 283

   HIKE Mantra — 284
   CARE Mantra — 286
   HEAL Mantra — 288
   TRUST Mantra — 290
   VIABLE Mantra — 292
   BREATH Mantra — 294
   JEDI Mantra — 296
   SUCCEED Mantra — 298
   KOAN Mantra — 300

Gratitude — 303
About the Author — 306
About the Business — 307
koanmethod.com — 308
Reading List — 309

Dedication

To Martin and Helyn for being my greatest teachers and growing my heart ten sizes, and to all the sister-friends who have held me with love and grace from breakdown to breakthrough.

Without you, none of this would have been possible.

... I grew up on the Great Lakes and recognize a seaworthy vessel when I see one. Regarding awakened souls, there have never been more able crafts in the waters than there are right now across the world. And they are fully provisioned and able to signal one another as never before in the history of humankind.

... Look out over the prow; there are millions of boats of righteous souls on the waters with you. In your deepest bones, you have always known this is so.

... If you are still standing, ragged flags or no, you are able. Thus, you have passed the bar. And even raised it. You are seaworthy.

... Ours is not the task of fixing the entire world all at once, but of stretching out to mend the part of the world that is within our reach.

... One of the most calming and powerful actions you can do to intervene in a stormy world is to stand up and show your soul.

Soul on deck shines like gold in dark times.

When a great ship is in harbor and moored, it is safe, there can be no doubt. But ... that is not what great ships are built for.[1]

~Clarissa Pinkola Estés, PhD

The First Step

The KOAN method begins from the premise that today's challenges require solutions that our current systems are not designed to produce repeatedly or reliably. It proposes a new model for cultivating Kind, Open, Adaptive Networks that foster and promote the kind of inclusion from which genuine creativity and innovation are born. It is also an invitation to sit, in the tradition of working with a Zen koan, in the uncertainty of not-knowing long enough, and with sufficient curiosity, for real breakthroughs to find us.

This book is 30 years in the making, but also written from a unique moment in history. Trying to write something that presumes to be timeless in these divided times seems both unhelpful and at odds with the spirit of **the KOAN method** itself.

This book is not about new things. In fact, in many ways, it is about very old things.

I am not the first to have explored these principles either. Many people have written about the ideas that I will touch on in these pages in much greater depth than I intend to. I am grateful for their work and the ways in which it has shaped me.

I began exploring questions of connection across differences in the 1990s, and first wrote about them in detail in my dissertation,[2] which was defended in April of 2001—just a few months before the attacks of September 11. So many pieces of that research have held up remarkably well over the years. In fact, if you were to read parts of it today, you might be surprised to realize how long ago it was written. Yet, as with anything written at a comparatively younger time in life and looked back on decades later, there are things in it that feel incomplete and even naïve to me now. My own understandings have evolved with time and experience.

In some ways that is precisely the point.

I didn't wait until I had it all figured out to begin.

I grew up moving back and forth between cultures, in a world that was always bigger than me. Human hopes, dreams, wants, and needs looked remarkably similar the world over, but our ways of helping, healing, hating, and harming one another wore many faces. We all had our own crossroads to contend with. In my early adulthood, Gloria Anzaldúa's poem "Borderlands"[3] captured this spirit for me:

> *To survive the Borderlands*
> *you must live sin fronteras*
> *be a crossroads.*

I grew up attending Civil Rights rallies and marching to Take Back the Night. I wrote my first letter to the editor opposing racism when I was 18 and was hosting interracial dialogue groups soon thereafter. I worked in group homes with young women who'd been court-removed from their families for being poor, or for not having a community of support, or because they were from the "wrong part of town." I saw how deeply all manner of institutions drew those divisions even more starkly along racial lines. I witnessed how systems were skewed in ways that could swallow people whole. My commitment to building more just systems was born early and has deep roots.

I was also born with white skin, in a country and cultural context where that mattered far more than anyone cared to admit in the 1970s and 1980s (and still does in many overt and covert ways). Even if I didn't come from great wealth, I certainly came from comfort and convenience and ease and access. Generations of my ancestors were college-educated, including a few of the women. We owned little bits of land and real estate in places where their value has grown steadily over decades.

As a white woman coming of age at the turn of the 21st century in America, I experienced everything that my generation of "emancipated" women enjoyed: I played sports, had easy access to birth control, had credit in my own name, could work, have babies, pay the bills, clean the dishes, and also experience sexual harassment, discrimination, and assault, all while showing up with a smile and not missing a beat alongside so many other successful professional women.

I had a complicated relationship with the intersection of my identities as I always lived a little bit between worlds. Ultimately, my curiosity about the things that tend to divide us, and how we relate to them, called me to graduate school. I studied the relationship between diversity and community-building and wrote about the making of what I called "Multi-vocal Culture," where different ideas and perspectives shaped a shared experience.

I have continued to teach university courses in communication, organizational culture, diversity, dialogue, community-building, social-movements, and leadership; and have looked far beyond my own field to understand these issues academically, interpersonally, and spiritually.

I have also worked with leaders in organizations of all sizes and now lead *Integrated Work* (integratedwork.com), a certified B Corp (bcorporation.net) that is part of a global community committed to harnessing the power of business as a force for good. We have been woman-owned and woman-led since 1998, and have intentionally and proactively cultivated a team that is more than 65% racial and ethnic minority. We are also testing the potential of self-organizing, distributed leadership, and are actively exploring employee-ownership models. We are re-imagining how we live, work, and lead together daily.

There still aren't many good maps for the kind of human-first, pro-justice future we believe is necessary to help us solve the enduring challenges of health equity, fair access to education, economic prosperity, and environmental protection that will be the hallmarks of a flourishing future for us all, so connecting with fellow travelers is important every day.

Many brilliant scholars, artists, and masters-of-their-craft of all kinds have shaped the thinking in these pages. I have intentionally chosen references and quotations from a wide range of people across cultures and from a wide range of ideologies. You may find that you identify or resonate more deeply with some than others. I hope the ones you might bristle at are as thought-provoking as the ones you find affinity with.

If you want to dive deep into any of the ideas that I will talk about (and I hope that you will because much of this bears exploring deeply and thoughtfully), I've designed the bibliography to be a treasure trove of wisdom and a reading list for the ages. The whole thing, with additional commentary on the texts and links to the readings and videos and resources I reference, as well as other tools, can be found at *koanmethod.com*.

What makes this book unique, and uniquely suited to this particular moment in history, is that it ties together things that the industrial age and the age of enlightenment tore apart. Some of that tearing and parsing and slicing and dicing yielded amazing insights and discoveries that helped humans better understand and see how the parts and pieces of our inner and outer universes were put together. Those insights spawned innovations that have extended lifespans, fueled innovation, and pulled millions of people out of poverty.

Somewhere along the way, though, we forgot that none of the bits were ever meant to function all on their own, that the true purpose of understanding any of it was always for the way we might discover to make it all work better together.

I've spent a significant fraction of my adult lifetime looking at this question from all angles: **What helps us to build a common good and what gets in the way?**

This book is inherently and intentionally multi-cultural and multi-disciplinary[4] in its approach to leadership and organizing. It looks at the question of what motivates and inspires people to get great things done together from a variety of vantage points to create a more textured view of what brings out the best in people. Fundamentally, this project is not about breaking down and examining, it is about weaving and connecting. It honors the shoulders it stands on and tries to put the pieces together again.

Since you are here, thank you for caring enough to go looking for the breakthrough.

Thank you for not waiting to have it all figured out before beginning.

You've already taken the first step. Let's go.

What you're supposed to do when you don't like a thing is change it.

If you can't change it, change the way you think about it.

~Maya Angelou

Leading, Now

This book is both a call to action and a beacon of hope. It is written for anyone who finds themselves leading—by profession, by choice, or by accident.

Its core premise is that the moments when we find ourselves feeling that everything is at its most broken—when we are most at odds with those around us and least able to see the possibility of a solution—that is when we are closest to a breakthrough, if only we can stay in the conversation and be ok with not knowing.

Fundamentally, this is a book about hard things—or, more accurately, what we do in the face of hard things. Its goal is to help readers look at the challenges in front of them with a renewed sense that truly good solutions are not only possible but inevitable, if we tap into enough different perspectives and listen with enough genuine curiosity to get unstuck.

It begins with the belief that the innovation necessary to achieve real breakthroughs is already all around us. However, we haven't done a good enough job of creating the conditions for people, with the right set of disparate ideas, to understand that the missing piece might be sitting just on the other side of what feels like an intractable divide. Many of us haven't learned to react with curiosity in the face of differences and so have little experience with the power that discovering such breakthroughs can bring.

In a world that feels more divided than ever, finding lasting solutions will require a new kind of leadership—focused on building the organizations and systems that support and reward a different and better way of doing things. Breakthrough leaders are needed to get there.

The KOAN method is part memoir, part social analysis, and part field guide for navigating the conflicts all around us. The central point of the book is that it is time to build a better way of leading and organizing that produces environments where creativity and innovation thrive.

You may find that you connect with certain parts of the book more easily than with others, and it is worth noticing what immediately resonates. I also invite you to pay attention to the parts that make you more uncomfortable or are harder to understand on first read. Those may also hold important insights for you (maybe about the ideas themselves and maybe about yourself and the way you relate to conflict or differences).

When something challenges your current thinking, do you pull back and disagree, or do you lean in and get curious?

Written primarily for business and nonprofit leaders, educators, policymakers, and concerned citizens, this book will also be helpful to anyone who wishes desperately to be more connected with those with whom they disagree, or who is struggling to find genuinely creative solutions to seemingly intractable problems.

Across all spheres of our lives, living **the KOAN method** in practice produces breakthrough magic.

This book makes the case that a new way of leading and organizing, one that connects us across our differences, is essential to solving today's biggest challenges, and offers concrete, easy-to-remember guidance to keep you centered, resourced, and able to navigate the twists and turns of a dynamic world.

This work is an effort to connect, synthesize, and integrate theories of leadership, organizing, transformation, and what we know about humans and how we are wired and interact, into a coherent method that others might choose to explore alongside me.

If you accept that invitation, you will learn the habits of mind and behavior that produce breakthrough leadership and discover practices and principles to help you get, and return, to that place in an often turbulent and divided world.

I call these *mantras* because they are not hard and fast rules or exact tools, but rather memory devices to sit with and reflect on. They are framed as sets of questions tied to a word or phrase that, I hope, will be easy to remember when the pull of the past has us stuck and we need a reminder that the future is ours to build.

Wherever you are as you pick up this book, I hope that, by the time you are done exploring the material here, you will feel a little lighter, find a renewed sense of optimism, and see more clearly what steps you can take to move from a place of division and discord to one where connection, co-creation, and common-good outcomes are the norm.

Chapter One

A World Divided

When you have a conflict, that means that there are truths that have to be addressed on each side of the conflict.

~Dolores Huerta

We are living in trying times, there's no question about it. Still just emerging from a global pandemic that killed millions of people around the world, and which fundamentally disrupted how we live, work, and are in community with one another, some days everything just feels BROKEN.

Inequities in our existing systems have come more and more into plain view and we've been given a chance to call into question whether the structures and philosophies that fueled industrial growth in the 20th century are well-suited to the much more rapidly evolving, complex, dynamic, and connected times we are living in now.

Even before the COVID-19 pandemic plunged the world into a shared global experiment, the early decades of the 21st century were testing the limits of industrial-age models as globalization made trade more interdependent[5] and as geopolitical conflicts caused mass migration and generated strong feelings on either side of immigration debates.[6,7] The (inter)national racial reckonings of the early 2020s also reinforced the sense that 20th-century systems had woven inequality into their fabric in material ways that we had not yet resolved satisfactorily. Meanwhile, the proliferation of digital social networks made it more possible than ever to affiliate with niche groups who shared an ideology,[8] even across vast distances, making it both easier to connect with people we may never actually meet in person and deepening the divisions between us.[9]

The cover of the March–April 2022 issue of *Harvard Business Review* featured the title "Managing a Polarized Workforce," and the titular article showed readers how to foster debate and promote trust by examining three core myths about conflict:[10] that people who disagree with us do so because they are uninformed or unintelligent, that disagreement will make people defensive, and that disagreement is inherently bad.

In fact, psychologists call this fear that engaging with difference will lead to breakdowns *false polarization*.

What if I told you that being polarized was the first step in the direction of innovation?

Is it possible that the search for common ground is the very thing that gets in the way of building a common good?

Many well-intended studies and leadership manuals tell us that being good at "managing difference" requires that we "seek points of agreement" or "teach people to be open-minded" and find a way to "get to yes."

A simple web search of any of these terms will yield lots of tips and tricks, but over and over again we are disappointed with the results. Often, the hunt for unobjectionable solutions only has us arrive at some mediocre middle-ground result. It might not provoke outright protest, but it doesn't generate any excitement or get to the heart of the underlying problem either.

This happens when common ground = least common denominator—when we settle for the least objectionable of the things we already know, but never get to discover anything new. True breakthrough ideas come from amplifying differences, not minimizing them. Much of my academic research focused on this key idea: that "radical encounters with otherness"[11,12,13] are essential to coming up with new ideas.

My decades of working in and with organizations all over the globe have also borne this out: If you want to understand something, you must MAGNIFY the distinctions, but also create the conditions in which they can be understood and made sense of. We've been hardwired to avoid, and even fear, the unfamiliar. But the world we live in and the challenges we must solve together require something new of us. Just as we have learned to harness technology to increase the size of our brains and the speed at which we can solve complex technical problems, we've got to learn to rewire our biology in ways that allow us to bring empathy and curiosity to differences so that we can heal festering wounds and solve the equally complex (and no less important) social challenges in front of us.

The irony is that the way to mutual understanding is THROUGH our differences, not around them or over them or instead of them. The quest for common ground breaks down when we try to skip the part where we really listen to each other. The experience of unity, community, and belonging is strongest when we embrace, explore, and amplify differences rather than erasing or managing them. AND, leaning into differences with real empathy helps us see the pieces that allow us to generate truly co-creative solutions.

This is easier said than done, though, and this book is intended to be a journey of un-learning the habits that no longer serve us so that we can build a better way, together.

As renowned activist and feminist scholar bell hooks said, "forgiveness and compassion are always linked: how do we hold people accountable for wrongdoing and yet at the same time remain in touch with their humanity enough to believe in their capacity to be transformed?"[14]

The answers to our challenges will rarely come from external factors but rather by looking within ourselves, digging into the heart of the conflict itself, and discovering the potential inherent in groups of people to come up with their own best solutions.

I'd been thinking about this question of building a common good for some time when I came across this tiny piece of writing from another time. Roughly 350 years ago, the Zen poet Basho wrote this haiku about calming the sway in our lives through connection:

> *now the swinging bridge*
> *is quieted with creepers*
> *our tendrilled life*

In reading it, I was struck that it is in fostering networks of connection that we "stay the sway" in our lives. When we stand on one side of an issue with the fear that the other side winning means we lose, the ground between us feels shaky and uncertain.

In the years I have spent studying and working shoulder to shoulder with people striving to bridge their differences, fostering connection is the only thing I've seen that creates both truly innovative solutions and the conditions for something that goes beyond "getting along."

The presence of difference, and the contrast it creates, helps us see things more clearly.

Choices and distinctions become sharper.

Suddenly, we have options.

Granted, the first step is often the hardest. By unlearning the things that no longer serve us, we can more intentionally choose strategies that are better suited to the times and challenges in front of us.

Lao Tzu was a revered Chinese master, writing nearly 2000 years ago. He is the person to whom the quote "a journey of a thousand miles begins with a single step" is most often attributed. For me, the spirit of this saying is that to do anything new, we must shift from complacency into action—from standing still to taking that first step.

So, before we go further on our learning journey, let's explore for a minute how we learn (and unlearn) so that we can begin to build something new, together.

We always take the first step from right where we are, and getting clear about where exactly that is, is what enables us to begin.

Begin the Journey

In my research and in my experiences all over the world, I have consistently seen that when you value and celebrate differences, you build bonds of trust and get better outcomes. When you minimize differences, solutions are of a lesser quality and are short-lived.

I've come to look at conflict as an indicator that creativity has not yet been sufficiently unleashed to integrate the various points of view at play. We are good at believing our own opinion and seeing the downside of someone else's.

Lots of great work on this notion of "polarity thinking" has been developed over the last several decades by Dr. Barry Johnson[15,16] and others.[17,18] These works highlight that there is often wisdom on both sides of an issue and that all knowledge is partial and incomplete without the benefit of other perspectives. Dr. Johnson's work emphasizes that, when confronted with difference, our job is not to challenge or contradict opposing views, but to supplement them so that we might all develop a more complete picture or robust understanding of a tension or paradox.

From this perspective, opposition isn't something to overcome but is an opportunity to enlarge our understanding of something. To get beyond the certainty that we have it all figured out and into the curiosity of what we might still be missing, we have to take that first step into the discomfort of not knowing.

In truth, that step is only uncomfortable to the extent that we are unpracticed at it. Most ancient wisdom traditions include some version of developing a "beginner's mind" as a steppingstone on the path to enlightenment.

As Gloria Steinem said, "The first problem for all of us . . . is not to learn but to unlearn."[19]

Learning is much more dynamic than what many stages-of-learning models portray—that we move in steady, progressive, mostly linear steps from not-knowing to some form of mastery.

I like to think about learning as a journey and remind myself that it is always active. The goal is not to know exactly where we will end up before we even begin, but to prompt ourselves to take that first step and to recognize, acknowledge, and even appreciate that, all along the way, we are building new tomorrows.

From *Hubris to Humility*, from *Insight to Inquiry*, from *Knowledge to Kinship*, and from *Effective to Embodied*, the HIKE mantra reminds us of the steps on the journey toward a more connected form of wisdom.

The First Step: From Hubris to Humility. The beginning of any learning journey involves a shift from thinking that we already know to recognizing that we just might have something new to discover. This is important relative to any given topic, but perhaps even more important as a mindset or disposition.

Dr. Carol Dweck's pioneering work[20] on fixed vs growth mindsets highlights the way our beliefs about what is "given" or "the way things are" affects our ability to learn new things, grow, and adapt. Decades of research shows that when people with a fixed mindset face a challenge, they tend to experience success or failure as an indicator of self-worth. This is why many people avoid situations where they believe that they won't do well or look outside of themselves for reasons that explain a "failure."

I call this state hubris because it represents an over-identification with our ego and a fierce effort to protect a persona that is "talented," "expert," "credentialed," or "morally upstanding" in some specific way, as opposed to confronting what is required of us for our own growth and development.

People with a growth mindset[21], on the other hand, see a challenge as an opportunity to learn, grow, and change and may even seek out things that stretch or push them in uncomfortable ways. Over time, those individuals learn to learn and become more comfortable with not knowing because their identities aren't bound up with already knowing. These people have the humility to recognize that none of us have all the answers and that approaching challenges with curiosity helps us get smarter over time and helps the system become smarter too, as we lean into exploring the unknown. As Dr. Dweck says, "It's not always people that start out the smartest that end up the smartest."

This first step from the hubris of defending what we already know to the humility of acknowledging that our piece of the puzzle is only one of many is critical to discovering breakthroughs on any topic but also valuable on the road to becoming a more agile leader, able to adapt and respond to changing conditions.

The Next Step: From Insight to Inquiry. As we begin to develop a new understanding of things, we grow curious and seek out more information, ideally from a wide range of perspectives. Once we have taken these first steps into a new mindset of curiosity, we tend to rapidly develop new insights about a given issue or dilemma. The trick is not to rush to closure too quickly. The point is not to move from one certainty to a new one, but to move from a place where options are limited to a field of possibilities where anything is imaginable. As the 13th-century Persian poet Rumi said, "Out there beyond right-doing and wrong-doing, there is a field. I'll meet you there."[22]

Bestselling authors and scholars Edgar and Peter Schein have coined the term *humble inquiry*[23] to refer to a model of leadership rooted in asking rather than in telling. This approach, they argue, is key to building more positive relationships and better organizations because it makes the whole system smarter. When leaders embrace the humility of not-knowing and lean into inquiry, they create the conditions for more people to speak up when things aren't working, suggest ideas that might solve intractable problems, and bring their best thinking forward. They foster inclusion.

As my own leadership has grown and evolved over the years, I've learned how important it is to surround myself with people who will challenge me and tell me truths I might not always want to hear. Some of the most successful leaders have emphasized that the secret to their success was to surround themselves with people smarter than they were in important ways—and with people who offered fresh perspectives. Crediting these people for their contributions also expands our sense of who can lead, and from where, in important ways.

Shifting to a mode of inquiry can be exhilarating and liberating if we let it. We no longer live in a world where the smart-person-at-the-top model works. The amount of information available to anyone, anywhere, at any time has proliferated in ways that make those who gather and synthesize input from many sources much more valuable than those who advocate fiercely for what they already know.

Going Deeper: From Knowledge to Kinship. A powerful shift happens when we make the move from understanding something conceptually to identifying with and internalizing it more fully. When we shift from having new insight about something to *belonging* to the idea in a different way, something magical begins to happen. I've been researching and writing about the art of community-building[24,25] for nearly 25 years and have constantly seen that when we begin to feel a part of, instead of apart from, an idea, that is when inspiration, innovation, and co-creation begin to show up.

Meg Wheatley has built an impressive body of work around the idea that there is tremendous power in "turning to one another" to restore hope and create the conditions for possibility.[26] Her work reminds us that all change begins from a place of caring enough to step out of complacency; and that when communities discover common cause and a shared vision of what is possible, they are a force of nature.

Mia Birdsong's powerful work on belonging and showing up for one another[27] is achingly beautiful. In it, she paints a revealing picture of the divides we have created, not only along lines of race and class and gender, but anywhere where we have forgotten that the cornerstone of the best human achievements has always been community. The in-it-togetherness of belonging is what motivates us to keep going when things are hard, and it is what makes us feel less lonesome along the way.

The important shift that happens at this point in our learning journey is that we acknowledge that we are not alone, and that to get anything important done we will have to find a way to do it together. This shift from knowing something to feeling kinship with, and belonging to it, transforms a theoretical exercise into a passion, a mission, or a devotion. Some people find their "calling" here.

When we recognize ourselves as interconnected and interdependent, we remember that our destinies are bound up in one another's. If I "win" at your expense, I've only contributed to a more divided world. When we begin to feel real kinship with the issues, ideas, and plights of our neighbors, coming up with solutions that serve us all becomes a compulsion, and curiosity begins to blossom.

A Living Practice: From Effective to Embodied. Mastery begins to bloom when we move beyond having an ability to *do* something to living the wisdom in-action and *being* an example of it. This is a hard thing to wrap one's head around in a world of top-five tips and how-to guides. And it's perhaps hard to understand in the ways we've become accustomed to, because embodied wisdom lives *in the body* (and the heart specifically) more than in the mind.

Really staying present to what we are feeling, how we are being affected, and how those effects influence our leadership takes intentionality and practice. New insights and expanded knowledge can inspire us to do the work of becoming more embodied leaders, but for those of us who have been conditioned to trust our intellect at the expense of our intuition, the shift from competent, capable, and effective to *embodied* tends to be the most challenging of these shifts.

The practices that get us there are not new—the Tao Te Ching, Bhagavad Gita, Four Noble Truths, canonical and mystical texts from the Abrahamic traditions (Judaism, Christianity, Islam, and their offshoots) as well as indigenous stories and lore from all corners of the world are filled with stories and rituals aimed at *becoming* the teaching. While its origins are unclear, a quote that I have always appreciated in this spirit is "When the student is ready, the teacher will appear. When the student is really ready, the teacher will disappear. . . ."

Brené Brown has become renowned for her work on authenticity and vulnerability[28,29] and has literally mapped an *Atlas of the Heart*[30]—charting the way to wholehearted living and leading. Her decades of work show that to live an authentic life, we must be able to meet discomfort with curiosity and empathy, not numb out or run from it. To bond with and belong to communities with others, we must first learn to sit with ourselves.

Any time you find yourself stuck in certainty or attached to an outcome; the *HIKE mantra* can help you move into the kind of curiosity that gets you back in motion.

the KOAN method

HIKE Mantra

Feeling stuck or holding on to a solution that just isn't working is an indication that certainty is interfering with curiosity. This mantra reminds us that no matter where we are in a learning journey, there is always a first or next step to take.

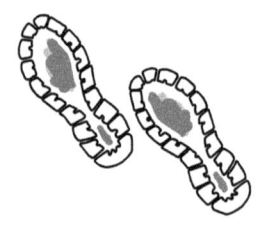

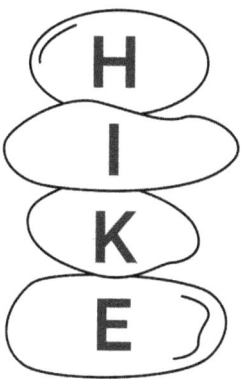

Where is *HUBRIS* holding me back?

How can I bring more *HUMILITY* to this question or challenge?

What *INSIGHTS* are challenging my old beliefs?

Where else can I be in intentional *INQUIRY* around this issue or question?

What new *KNOWLEDGE* am I acquiring; how is it changing me?

What *KINSHIP* do I feel with this issue; how am I already a part of it?

What does it look and feel like to be *EFFECTIVE* in this work?

How can I be more *EMBODIED* around this question; who lives this well?

The good news is that humans have thousands of years of practice using curiosity and ingenuity to move ourselves forward. There are traditions in all of our histories and lineages that can get us there. The challenging part, always, is having the humility to recognize that doing so is a worthy pursuit and then taking that first step on the journey.

The KOAN method is an invitation to that quest and a resource for everyone who is hungry to move beyond the things that divide us to forge a better way. There is plenty of practicality in these pages but there are no quick fixes that will allow you to skip the messy middle.

Though I've been a student and scholar of these questions for more than a quarter century, it's been my years of practice that have really shaped this work.

I've travelled the world, working with leaders across a wide range of organizations, facing myriad challenges, to build better teams and set clearer direction to find a way through crises of all kinds. Over decades, I have sat in circles of women, elders, and guides and spent meaningful solo (all-one[31]) time in nature.

This has been my crucible of transformation so, before we dive into the details of **the KOAN method**, I want to take you inside my own journey of unlearning.

Chapter Two

Alone in the Desert

I've been afraid every day of my life, but I've gone ahead and done it anyway.

~Georgia O'Keefe

Long before I got to the desert, I was shaped by the ocean.

I was born and raised on both sides of the Atlantic and spent months and months at the shore in my early years—looking out at a horizon that seemed to go on and on endlessly.

The year I turned eight, my family moved overseas, and I got my first vivid taste of how bullies can rule the school. Over the next six years, I moved back and forth between neighborhoods and across continents, in a near-constant state of being "the new kid." I learned early on that people tend to respond to differences in one of two ways—either by trying to make them go away or by becoming interested and curious. I've spent my life trying to be the latter and it has often felt like I was going against the grain.

As I grew into adulthood, questions about where and how our differences enhanced and enlivened our lives, instead of fraying them, fueled the choices I made about what to study, where to work, when to stay, and when to go.

Early in my career I was often the first, only, or youngest woman in the room and spent the earliest years of the 21st century trying to figure out how to "have it all"[32,33] when much of the workforce was seeing stable, well-paying jobs evaporate in favor of temperamental service or gig work. The more successful I became on the surface, the less **connected** I felt to friends, family, and, sometimes, even to my own heart. The rules of the game didn't leave much room for my embodied humanity and, by the time I was in my late 30s, the realization dawned that if I wanted sisterhood, kinship, or sounding boards that would tell me the truth with care, I would need to go and find and cultivate them.

My work has been made so much richer because I listened to that call.

I've found those communities of amazing humans in many circles since then, but one of my first sisterhoods began at the Center for Nature and Leadership over a decade ago. Since then, I've spent a lot of time in the wild, learning to listen differently and more deeply.

Sometimes on those journeys, I bring a journal and let the land I am on help me to remember, integrate, and process my story.

I share this excerpt as an insight into some of the moments and experiences that have inspired me to write this book, and as an example of the synthesis that becomes possible when we stop forcing and find flow.

Ghost Ranch, NM
May 2022

I settled in and leaned back, trying to get comfortable as I surveyed the vast landscape of New Mexico sprawling before me.

Red rocks spread out in every direction, and above me was the bluest sky dotted by just a few wisps of white clouds on the horizon. It all felt so familiar to me now.

So many hard and heavy things were swirling in my head. I worried that I'd be restless and not able to find the inner quiet I had come here looking for.

I closed my eyes against the sun and was flooded with a memory from another time and place—my thoughts took me back to a hotel room in Melbourne, Australia, ten years prior.

Light had filtered in through the crack in the curtain as I tried to shake myself awake after a long flight from Beijing and an endless series of client meetings the day before.

I could still feel the weight of the thought I'd had in that room a decade earlier, "What was I even doing here?"

In China, the air had been so thick with smog that people wore masks in public or avoided going outside all together whenever possible. The commuters riding their bicycles down the wide boulevards had special respirators to filter out the soot as they zipped along. Yet, there were also those who gathered in the park to do Tai Chi, as they always had, repeating age-old movements in silent flow despite the haze of pollution all around them.

I had been in China to help a group of NGO leaders craft a plan to influence the then-new administration to be bold in its clean energy goals. Even on the short walk from the hotel to their offices, it was hard not to feel like the battle had already been lost.

Just before boarding my plane from China to Australia, my phone pinged to reveal a picture of my young children, sent by their father—wildfire smoke billowing on the ridge behind them in Boulder, Colorado. He was holding down the fort at home while I was away on yet another business trip.

The smog in Beijing and the fires in my own backyard collided in ways that made it hard not to see the interconnectedness of it all. The kids were ok, their dad assured me, but it was little consolation to this not-yet-40 working mom who was more than 6,000 miles away from home.

On landing in Melbourne, I headed straight into meetings with a large telecom company (in the business of connection) that was trying to improve its image with customers.

The Skype call I had tried with the family when I got to my hotel later that evening had been the usual debacle, though. The time zones were always just too far off, and the connection never quite good enough. It was mostly just frustrating for everyone on the line.

I was tired, missed my family, and felt like I was moving grains of sand with a pair of tweezers most days. And the sun had seemed to be taunting me as it came through that hotel window—reminding me that I was already late for something.

Back in the present, sitting under a little juniper in the desert, I was surprised to feel a catch in my throat at remembering how hard it had been to try to talk to my little ones from so far away, all those years ago. Early versions of video calls had often meant broken speech and delayed pictures and nearly impossible conversations with toddlers and grade-schoolers, not to mention with the father who was left behind to wrangle them.

I felt the tangle of all the things I had missed in those many years on the road, alongside the opportunities both I, and they, had had because of those choices. Choices that often had felt like no choice at all—the only thing to be done with the hand I had been dealt. Our globally connected world often felt like it was fraying at the seams as I tried to hold it all together.

As I shaded my eyes again against the New Mexico sun, I remembered the other sting of that long-ago trip—being in business meetings full of men who'd been taught over the course of their entire lives that their voices were important, that having the last word was how the game was won, and that being (and staying) on top of the power pile was an end unto itself.

I winced as I recalled too many dismissive, demeaning, and disappointing conversations with leaders who managed to make the rooms they were in less intelligent, less creative, and less caring. For the most part, these were "good people" who thought highly of themselves and were successful by most measures; but the systems they had climbed their way to the top of were designed to have many more losers than winners, and self-deception was woven into the fabric of those worlds.

To succeed in extractive industries built on getting the most of anything, one had to be willing to believe that building a world full of people who chronically got less could somehow add up to victory without exacting a terrible cost.

How many years had I put up with that toxicity, believing there had to be a better way?

I opened my eyes for a minute, shaking my head at the thought. For so long I'd let my voice be silenced or my work be diminished (or claimed by someone else). I had missed sporting and school events and more bedtimes than I cared to count. I had sacrificed my own health and sanity by taking the earliest or latest flights, so that I could split myself in two (or three, or 10), trying to satisfy everyone and never quite succeeding.

As a large cloud moved in front of the desert sun, I felt a chill and shivered, remembering how early the experience of being picked on and shut out had started. I shifted positions, curling up against the wind, reassuring the little girl in me who could still remember the feeling of her patent leather shoes scuffing on the pavement and wearing tights over the scabs on her knees from all the fighting and falling on the hardscrabble playground of my French schoolyard.

It never ceases to amaze me how sights, smells, or sounds can take us right back into a memory we couldn't have conjured in quite the same way if we tried. How the bank teller or grocery clerk reminds us of a favorite (or feared) aunt or teacher or boss. How we go back to foods our grown-up selves might not otherwise care for because they remind us of our grandmother or a long-lost summer. Those habits of memory can both help us and hook us—keep us grounded and steady or hold us stuck.

Here, now, in the at once beautiful and rugged desert landscape, I could feel the tug of sun and shade, heat and cold; and with both, I reveled in how far I had come since those moments my memory had served up and how long the road ahead still seemed. I'd been coming to this place in the desert for nearly a decade, finding community with an amazing group of women who I had actively searched for when I realized that my male business partners were never going to be a source of sisterhood. Finding my strength and my voice required me to create my own community and find my own containers of care in which to blossom.

The global COVID-19 pandemic had caused so much pain and heartache and death, but it had also created a glimmer of hope that we might build something new and different and better. Taken-for-granted ways of doing everything from school, to work, to gathering with friends and family, to moving people and goods around the world, had been disrupted overnight.

Where a decade ago I could barely read my kids a bedtime story over Skype, I was now running a global business via Zoom all day every day. We'd seen the starkly different impacts on health and well-being in different communities with different resources. "Impossible" solutions had been developed at record speed, but conflict also simmered below the surface, and we were as divided as we had ever been in many ways.

I felt both the urgency and the opportunity of the moment.

We were living in such polarized times—the chasms between people and the distance to solving increasingly pressing challenges seemingly got greater by the day. Yet somehow, I was growing more hopeful. The differences that needed to be reconciled were so close to the surface now, so visible in plain sight, that not solving them seemed unthinkable.

I checked the time and sat up, looking around at the landscape made iconic by Georgia O'Keefe almost a century ago, marveling at how it was becoming home to me after the many trips I had now made here. What had once felt surprising and strange, and even a little foreboding, was now familiar and I had grown to love it.

It struck me that that was, perhaps, what was at the heart of what I'd been grappling with.

As I started to pack up my little camp chair and took a swig of water, getting ready to head back to the group of wise women who were becoming more like family with each of our gatherings, the threads of the stories I'd just been remembering seemed to braid themselves together into precisely the kind of clarity I'd hoped to find.

I could see that, always, when some conflict or division had been overcome, it had been by learning to love the things that had once felt strange or "wrong." And, it had always come from a willingness to connect with others in search of answers. I had written about this just before the pandemic with a friend and fellow entrepreneur who was doing her own great work to grow heart-centered leaders.[34] I laughed a little out loud at the reminder. I put my water bottle in my pack and picked up my journal to scribble one last line, "leverage the power of 'we.'"

It felt more relevant of an idea than ever.

As I slung my day pack over my shoulder, I could feel all the bumps in the road that had led me here and could sense that, as far as I had come, the shift that was beginning to take root also meant that the journey was just beginning or entering a new chapter.

Chapter Two—Alone in the Desert

As I walked back to the group, a poem I had written the year before, during the peak of the pandemic, came to mind and I thought of reading it for our closing circle that afternoon.

This is that poem.

Chapter Two—Alone in the Desert

Poetic Pause
A Stirring

Most everything that matters
Is preceded
By a stirring so subtle
That it may go unnoticed

Unless one knows
To listen
For its low hum
Of foreshadowing

The stirring is meant
To heighten the senses
Attune one's attention
So that the thing is not missed

But, ironically
We so often get
Caught up in the
Turbulence itself

That we miss
Its very reason for being
We avoid the tumult
Distance ourselves from discord

Believing that achieving peace
Demands calm
When the converse
Is true

The calm that comes before
The storm

the KOAN method

Is no match for the deep
Stillness that follows it

To anyone who takes the time
To notice, the former
Is a placid tension
Fraught with unexpressed conflict

One ought be wary
Of that version of calm
For it portends
Volcanic eruption

As the
Subterranean
Pressure builds before
Finally breaching containment

Those, however
Who dare ride the wave
Of mystery
Find an altogether different peace

This calm lives deep within
Is nurtured in surrender
Not suppression
And is always in the now

Present
Aware
Alive
Being

The journey
To the latter
Traverses the former
Refusing to abide there

As we try to reimagine our way forward in a still-divided world, it will be helpful to remember that the stirring of discomfort is not the problem itself, but a signal that we are in the presence of difference, and that that is the birthplace of innovation.

That is where breakthroughs are born.

Chapter Three

Why the KOAN method?

I'd love to give you something but what would help?

~Ikkyu, Crow with No Mouth

So, why **the KOAN method**?

A koan is a paradoxical riddle or story that has no "answer" and isn't meant to be "understood." Its purpose is to show the seeker that no amount of logical reasoning or problem-solving will get us to nirvana, or enlightenment. Simple examples include "what is the sound of one hand clapping?" and "if a tree falls in a forest with no one to hear it, does it make a noise?" But some are longer parables and stories that must be peeled back, layer by layer.

A koan is intended, quite literally, to "break your brain" by confronting it with an irreducible paradox that can only be resolved through surrender to its both-and-ness. It's designed to startle you awake and reminds us that separateness is fiction and that we are all in this together.

This disposition to sitting with paradox, instead of trying to get one side to come out on top, always helps to remind me that win-lose models ALWAYS have more losers than winners and that winning today just means you have a target on your back tomorrow.

Embarking on a journey to achieve something big and important, to truly make an impact, is a worthy goal but can be challenging, too. We understand the key ingredients: setting a course, inspiring people to bring their individual best to achieve it, helping them feel a part of a broader common cause, and improving everyone's circumstance in the process.

Most of the time, though, these outcomes come with serious setbacks and twists and turns along the way. Lofty ambitions run into the practicalities of everyday life; real commitment to a cause devolves into antagonism, apathy, and/or attrition. When things get hard, people get angry or give up. The stress and lack of productivity in these situations often has the most thoughtful among us not wanting to even bother.

The irony is that, as with most things in life that matter, that moment of friction or frustration, when tensions seem to be at their highest, is the very moment when the breakthrough is closest at hand. If only we can stay in the discomfort long enough, and with enough curiosity, to find it. In *Theory U: Leading from the Emerging Future*, C. Otto Scharmer makes the case that the pace and complexity of today's world demands leaders who can sense and respond to their environment dynamically and that the most important leadership skill might be the ability to "listen to the whole better than anyone else."[35]

Yet, history, culture, and biology have primed us to attack or avoid things that aren't familiar or "don't make sense." What was adaptive for survival thousands of years ago is poorly suited to the ever-changing and highly interconnected world in which we now live.

Where we once could live out the bulk of our lives in relatively confined geographies, interacting mostly with people from the same families, tribes, and clans, today we are able to travel the world and, whether we choose to venture far afield or not, we interact with people at great distances and with vastly different backgrounds and experiences every day through the media we consume, the products we buy, and/or the professions we pursue.

That means we need divergent thinking to solve the challenges we face and the once-adaptive fight-flee-freeze-fawn response is now often an act of self-sabotage, getting in the way of achieving the positive progress and outcomes we want and need.

I've spent the last several decades studying organizations and how they operate; working alongside some of the biggest and most recognized brands in the world as well as with some of the most underserved communities. It turns out that most of the challenges humans face aren't that different whether you are working with a multinational bank, a local environmental or educational nonprofit, a media giant, or a community health center providing safety-net care to the underinsured.

Getting good work done together boils down to a few key things: our ability to listen and act empathetically (**Be Kind**); to trust people with information that impacts their lives and affects their work (**Be Open**); to develop systems that are resilient and agile (**Be Adaptive**); and to lean into the relationships and partnerships required to meet our mission rather than building walls around our organizations (**Build a Network**). While some of us are good at doing some of these things some of the time, having all of them show up together happens all too rarely.

While we have invested a lot over recent decades in developing mission-driven leaders, we haven't sufficiently evolved our systems to keep up with the power and potential of that aspiration.[36] If we really want to achieve breakthrough results, getting past the intractability of the things that divide us and learning to build **Kind, Open, Adaptive Networks** of people joined together to get good things done will be the key to making a lasting shift.

The premise behind mission-driven, connected leadership is a good one. Rather than a small number of "smart" leaders defining goals, breaking them down into tasks, and doling them out to individuals who do what they are told, mission-driven leaders set a clear direction and inspire people to want to reach a common and meaningful goal. The creativity and motivation that this approach unlocks, especially for solving complex challenges, is far greater than any management style can produce.

This sentiment was captured sweetly by Antoine de Saint Exupéry, author of *The Little Prince*: "If you want to build a ship, don't drum up the men [sic] to gather wood, divide the work and give orders. Instead, teach them to yearn for the vast and endless sea."[37]

When we show people that they matter as humans and to the organization and its mission, they are more motivated to contribute in meaningful ways to reach shared goals.

This is **the KOAN method** in action.

The first step is the most straightforward but also the one that gets overlooked most often: **Be Kind**. Treating people like they matter, and meaning it, turns out to be one of the most powerful motivators at a leader's disposal. Dale Carnegie knew this more than 100 years ago when he wrote his now-renowned *How to Win Friends and Influence People*.[38] The organizations that have taken this notion deeply to heart tend to find that loyalty is greater, that engagement is higher, and that innovation flourishes.

For organizations that have cracked the kindness code, the next move is to go beyond "you matter" to "you matter to us." One of the best ways to do this is to increase transparency and openness, trusting people with the information that affects them and their work. **Being Open**, far more than parties and company picnics, influences feelings of belonging and connectedness. Organizations that have embraced pay transparency, for example, spend less time negotiating during hiring, tend to provide more meaningful performance feedback, do so more regularly, and grow their teams' capacity to engage in the kinds of challenging conversations that fuel real growth.[39]

People also want to know that their work matters to what their organization is up to. This isn't just about being in the know or satisfying people's FOMO (fear of missing out). When leaders help their team members connect the meaningfulness of their individual contributions to the overall vision and mission, they become more agile and can **Be Adaptive**. Rather than just doing their job, they can make contributions that continue to steer toward a collective goal even in the face of changing circumstances. As the pace of change increases and a dynamic environment makes detailed long-term planning more and more challenging, having people who see their role as helping to fulfill a purpose will prove far more valuable than those who see their job as completing more narrowly defined tasks or duties.

Even organizations that believe in the importance and power of mission and are willing to invest significantly in setting clear direction and engaging individual leaders in championing it can get in their own way if they ask leaders to operate in new ways inside of old systems. Most of the challenges in front of us won't be solved by one company, one country, or one community. Better solutions will arise more rapidly and readily as we perfect our ability to **Build a Network** around the challenges—to cultivate partners, listen to stakeholders, and see our contributions as part of a larger tapestry of effort and innovation.

When leaders embrace these principles, amazing things can happen.

Be Kind, Be Open, Be Adaptive, Build a Network.

Chapter Three—Why the KOAN method?

A KOAN Case Study: Embracing Innovation

In 2007, Jane Chen and three friends from grad school were working on a project for their Design for Extreme Affordability project at Stanford's Hasso Plattner Institute of Design (often referred to as the d. school). They had been challenged to design a solution to keep premature babies warm that cost less than 1% of the cost of a traditional incubator (then around $20,000 USD).

On a fact-finding trip to India and Nepal, they discovered that the obstacles to quality neonatal care were not just financial but also practical and cultural. There were lots of expensive and unused incubators in the hospitals in big cities but the state of roads between the cities and rural villages made travel unreasonable for fragile newborns and their mothers. AND baby-wearing and physical touch are so culturally integral to both maternal care and infant care that the thought of putting a tiny baby in a sterile container where they couldn't be touched or held wasn't viable.

Their solution: The Embrace Baby Warmer,[40] a sleeping bag with a pocket on the back to hold a warming device made of a space-age wax. This insert holds a stable temperature for four hours and can be warmed by simply dropping it in a pot of boiling water.[41] The cozy sleeping bag allowed tiny preemies to be swaddled and kept at just the right temperature at arm's length from their mothers in a cost-effective and culturally conscious way. Not only did Jane and her classmates achieve their company's design challenge, but they also launched a social-enterprise company that has helped save more than 350,000 premature babies across the developing world in the last decade.

Now, their sister company, Little Lotus[42] uses the same technology to create swaddling blankets for babies in the Global North, keeping babies' temperature regulated and helping them sleep better; and proceeds help defray the costs of Embrace Incubators using a buy-one-give-one model.[43]

I first learned about Jane on a visit to the d. school in 2014 when I was working on a project to help the leadership team of an international financial services firm explore models for purpose-driven leadership. I had the honor of meeting Jane and learning more about her story when she became one of the first U.S. firms funded by SheEO (now Coralus[44]), an innovative network building an alternative economy with regenerative capital (more on them later!).

Jane's story was inspiring because it modeled the power of human-centered design-thinking[45] in action. Rather than looking at a problem from a purely technical perspective, their team worked to understand the needs of the people most impacted by the problem and its solution, explore a wide range of potential options (including unconventional ones), then prototype, test, and iterate them to improve and refine their idea.

Empathize   Ideate   Prototype   Test   Iterate

Figure 1. Human Centered Design Process

The story was a compelling one—tiny babies, cultural sensitivity and curiosity, and a solution that leveraged both cutting-edge technology and ancient wisdom to solve a pressing problem in a simple and elegant way.

It also almost never happened.

After grad school, Jane and her co-founders moved to India to build the business, had early successes, and secured the funding they needed to scale. Ready to bring the company global, Jane had moved back to California when, just before her final investment was due to come in, her funder was acquired, and the deal was off. With only seven days of funding in the bank, she scarcely had time to panic before needing to find her way to a breakthrough.[46]

A longtime surfer and Zen meditation practitioner, Jane found her way to a solution in a very KOAN way.

The Embrace Baby Warmer is an innovation born from the sort of *Kindness* that is rocket fuel for creativity and innovation, deep empathy and listening to the community's needs, and getting past any hubris of knowing what the right answer should be to develop real kinship with the question in need of solving.

In being *Open* to having any preconceptions challenged and transparent in the design and development, the Embrace team cultivated creativity and truly innovative thinking.

That receptivity also helped them be *Adaptive* and pivot rapidly when the future, as they had planned for it, literally evaporated overnight.

Then, the *Network* they had cultivated with the d. school, with the people in the communities where their device was saving lives and healing families, with the space agencies and tech companies whose material was at the core of their product, and with the global partners and colleagues who believed in their invention, allowed them to put together the necessary resources in a short time and helped evolve the business model for sustainability.

This is what is possible when we develop our capacity to sit in the unknown long enough for breakthroughs to surface and then tend to the environment in which they can emerge.

The KOAN method gives us an alternative model, rooted both in ancient wisdom and cutting-edge research, to evaluate and evolve how we come together as humans to solve today's stickiest problems.

A Turning Point

So many of the ways we organized ourselves pre-pandemic became irrelevant overnight in early 2020. In some cases, we discovered that the things that once kept us connected and efficient actually accelerated the spread of the virus as it raced across the globe and disrupted life for everyone.

Now, as we try to find our footing in a "what's next" world, it has become clear that there really isn't any going back and that the solutions that got us to this turning point aren't at all suited to what's ahead. In her book **The Light We Carry**, Michelle Obama reflects on this time, saying, "It may be a while before we find our footing again. The losses will reverberate for years to come. We will get shaken and shaken again. The world will remain both beautiful and broken. The uncertainties aren't going away. But when equilibrium isn't possible, we are challenged to evolve."[47]

Hybrid work is likely here to stay. Those who are forcing a return to the office are being met with fierce resistance, resentment, and resignations from employees who now see that hours-long commutes and being under someone's direct physical supervision have little to do with the quality of their work. How we shop, play, and travel may look very different for some time to come.

How families and communities gather, celebrate, and organize are being reimagined. Problems like climate change, social justice, and global politics can't be solved in isolation. These are the moments that hold potential for real and lasting shifts in understanding and re-imagining of how the organizations that we put in place pre-COVID might evolve in this next era.

The KOAN method gives us a framework for evaluating the systems we're in today and evolving them to better meet tomorrow's needs. Getting there requires us to begin leaning into connection and cultivating curiosity in the face of differences.

The section that follows invites you into the next step on the journey, to challenge and explore these ideas more extensively as we take a deep dive into each element of *the KOAN method*:

- how to cultivate *Kind* cultures;
- how to foster *Open* systems;
- how to be *Adaptive*;
- how to nurture *Networks* of relationship.

In each chapter you will find a combination of research and examples that examine how and why each element of the method matters, coupled with stories, mantras, and case studies that illustrate the ideas in practice, and sprinkled with quotations and short passages of poetry and prose designed to periodically inspire, provoke, or nudge you out of any reverie.

At the end of the book the mantras are summarized in a tidy collection to support you on your journey to breakthrough leadership.

The KOAN method is both a practical framework and a state of mind.

Poetic Pause
Now, Empty Your Cup

The **Parable of the Tea** is one of my favorite Zen koans.

It goes like this:

Nan-in, a Japanese master during the Meiji era (1868–1912), received a university professor who came to inquire about Zen.

Nan-in served tea.

He poured his visitor's cup full, and then kept on pouring.

The professor watched the overflow until he no longer could restrain himself.

"It is overfull. No more will go in!"

"Like this cup," Nan-in said, "you are full of your own opinions and speculations. How can I show you Zen unless you first empty your cup?"

The state of interbeing is a vulnerable state.

It is the vulnerability of the naïve altruist, of the trusting lover, of the unguarded sharer.

To enter it, one must leave behind the seeming shelter of a control-based life, protected by walls of cynicism, judgment, and blame.[48]

~Charles Eisenstein

A Different Way

The KOAN method gives us both a framework and a set of practices for building a common good.

This model of leading and organizing, rooted both in ancient wisdom and cutting-edge research, can help us evaluate and evolve how we come together as wildly diverse humans to solve today's stickiest problems.

By imagining new models for living and organizing in *Kind, Open, Adaptive Networks*, we can radically reimagine the things that keep us stuck.

The chapters that follow take a deep dive into each of the elements, exploring the wisdom each holds for building bridges to create common good solutions.

We look at existing systems that are impersonal and disconnected and that rely on individual progress as markers of success; we also examine how we can build *kind* systems rooted in empathy, connection, and care.

We spotlight some of the still-in-place structures that were designed, sometimes intentionally and sometimes by accident, to confuse and obstruct—structures built on secrecy and withholding of information—and then look inside some fascinating organizations working to build more *open* systems that put the true power of trust in more people's hands.

We look at the tangle of bureaucratic crazy-making we have built around ourselves via rigid and inflexible rules in the name of standardization and scale and then explore exciting new models that are producing more nuanced and personalized systems that are *adaptive* and resilient in the face of an ever more dynamic world.

Finally, we look at places where people all over the world are clinging to clan-like identity groups as their source of security but discovering themselves less connected and more exposed than ever as we also marvel at the role of **networks** built on the art of reciprocity and mutual thriving.

We are living in extremely dynamic times and many of the systems we built for the industrial age are too cold, closed, constraining, and disconnected to solve the very real, very big, and very human challenges that affect us all.

Centuries of evolution have hardwired us to defend ourselves against perceived threats in order to perpetuate the species. Each of these "survival" strategies has their pitfalls, though. As French philosopher (and activist in the French Resistance during World War II) Simone Weil once said, "No matter what the circumstances, the worst betrayal will always be to subordinate ourselves to this apparatus and to trample underfoot, in its service, all human values in ourselves and in others."[49]

One source of this challenge lies in the ways we set up systems to reward, acknowledge, and appreciate some behaviors over others—often at the individual level—instead of weaving methods of self-and-other discovery into our ways of being and doing. These old habits get in the way of realizing the full potential of **the KOAN method**.

For decades, organizations have focused on being mission-driven as an individual set of leadership traits or aspirations at the expense of addressing the underlying systems, policies, and practices of organizing that are holdovers from the models described above.

So, we encourage collaboration and authentic communication but still reward people for personal performance, deception, and withholding. We say we want everyone to be treated the same, and hold out the carrot of merit pay, then measure and rank order people in ways that communicate loudly that there are "right" ways to operate and that some are better at it than others.

If we want to build solutions that work for more people more of the time, we have to confront the alignment of our ideals with models of structuring our organizations that recognize and reward these purpose-driven practices.

Having a clear and compelling mission matters more than ever today, especially as organizations work on increasingly complex issues that can't be easily "managed" or broken down into discrete tasks.

Getting our mission right, and steering true to it, has many well-known benefits: it reduces supervision costs by pointing the team toward a clear goal, it helps attract talent that cares about the things the team cares about, and it makes it easier for everyone to understand how the work they do matters.

What's more, we now have years of research telling us that these very benefits are the things that motivate performance in a knowledge economy. In the 1970s, Richard Ryan and Edward Deci began to elaborate on a theory of self-determination[50] that has been more recently evolved and popularized by authors such as Dan Pink,[51] Chip and Dan Heath,[52] Angela Duckworth,[53] and Marshall Goldsmith.[54]

The core premise of all of this work, and what I have applied and observed in practice for years, is that people take more ownership for their own experience, persist in their endeavors with greater resilience, and generate better outcomes for themselves and their organizations when they have a say in how work gets done, see the relationship between their contribution and something larger than themselves, and feel successful in their efforts.

Over the last few decades, many organizations have spent a lot of money for their leaders to learn mission-driven leadership. Then they've waited expectantly for the benefits of better employee performance (and thus higher profits) to roll in.

Many of them have been disappointed.

This isn't because the leaders failed at leading from mission and purpose, though. In most cases, that part of the experiment succeeded dramatically.

The problem is that most companies' organizational systems, structures, and policies haven't kept pace with the individual insights and aspirations in the C-suite. So, we have created a whole generation of leaders who aspire to do something more or different . . . but are left trying to apply what they have learned to organizations that were not designed to be led in a mission-driven way.

The models of organizing that grew out of the industrial revolution were designed to optimize assembly-line-style work that was good at producing all manner of widgets at scale. These hierarchical systems were built on notions of smart people at the top coming up with solutions and distributing tasks to a workforce that was considered largely unskilled.

As we have moved into an ever more knowledge-based economy, these methods of management just don't work as well and, even in today's manufacturing environments, we know that people work better when we take a human-first approach to leadership.

Yet too many organizations qualify their care in a way that sounds a lot like "you matter, but . . . not as much as XYZ (the bottom line, hitting your numbers, following the rules, being a team player . . .)." This shows up as systems with nice recruitment materials, a collection of enticing perks, and sometimes even a lot of transparency . . . but also a persistent set of rules and reward systems that are rigid, impersonal, or contradictory.

The effect of this has been to reduce autonomy, inhibit decision-making, and massively increase the cost of supervision. These systems have also failed to build the bonds of connection and community necessary to bring us together in the face of challenges or times of crisis.

We know that when individuals have some measure of control over how they spend their time and complete their tasks, their engagement increases, and they foster a greater sense of ownership. So why spend time and money on things that give people less influence and control over their own work? When the company line and lived experience don't match, people may initially feel inspired and encouraged, but they become demoralized and disillusioned when aspiration collides with reality.

This is made worse by day-to-day practices that communicate both subtly and overtly that "we don't really trust you." Many organizations still hold salaries so tightly that pay equity gets undermined and have bonus and incentive schemes that are unclear or hard to predict. These management methods lead to a feeling of arbitrariness that leave team members feeling at the mercy of senior leadership, tend to foster territoriality, create conditions in which people learn to "play the game" within a chain-of-command, and turn accountability into a kind of quid pro quo where employees learn to expect that "good" behavior comes with external rewards. The results not only get economically expensive over time but also cause employees to end up feeling a lack of belonging—isolated and inhibited rather than connected and committed.

The effect of this environment, then, is to create employees who don't really know how or why their contribution matters and, so, are willing to cut corners and do the bare minimum to get by. Why put in the extra effort when the best you can hope for is to get a pat on the back or a "prize" if the right person notices your efforts? The effect of all of this is that middle-layers of leadership feel disillusioned, and employees feel undervalued—all stuck in a Faustian bargain and unable to find the exit.

The double-edged sword here is that the leaders themselves often fail to recognize the paradoxes and tensions that their own mission-driven leadership creates. In many cases, the leader does care, does truly believe in the mission, and does genuinely want to engage their team in bringing a mission to life. But despite these honorable impulses, they can't quite navigate the systems, structures, and/or people who set goals and run operations in their own company.

Believing in the power of their own good intentions, these leaders can easily fall into a sort of benevolent dictator mode of operating.

Despite the persistence of impersonal policies and a lack of transparency due to systems and structures that companies have had in place for decades, leaders assume the mission will magically inspire everyone and everything to align with it. Then they're disappointed when their employees don't buy into the mission as much as they themselves have.

Whether you experience this as a leader or an employee in a large organization, or have felt it around your family dinner table, or at your parent-teacher meetings, it's worth learning to recognize when our survival strategies turn to self-sabotage.

In the chapters that follow, we'll go to work on building the systems we do want, exploring examples of things that interfere with the benefits that *the KOAN method* can bring, and look at the trailblazers and early adopters who are already out there beginning to build a bold new world.

First, let's look at why *Kind Cultures* are key to unlocking the creativity we need to solve the challenges wrought by division and disconnection.

You never change things by fighting the existing reality. To change something, build a new model that makes the existing model obsolete.[55]

~Buckminster Fuller

the KOAN method

cultivating **kind** cultures

fostering **open** systems

being **adaptive**

nurturing **networks** of relationship

Chapter Four

Cultivating Kind Cultures

People will forget what you said, people will forget what you did, but people will never forget how you made them feel.

~Maya Angelou

Many people who have experience with contemporary organizations and systems have a story or two (or ten) of something that either caused them harm or failed to show them care. Maybe you've been publicly challenged in a way that was more demeaning than constructive, experienced being ignored or talked over in a meeting, or been excluded or passed over for a promotion without explanation. Perhaps you've felt like you need to check your identity at the door or have experienced a thousand little cuts from comments or behaviors that ignore and diminish an important part of who you are. Most of us can point to a time when we had to miss an important event in our personal lives (from a doctor's appointment to a major family milestone) because of expectations at work.

For most of the 20th century, organizations of all kinds were built on a work/life separation framework. Leadership and managerial models like Scientific Management[56] and its heirs emphasized efficiency over humanity at work. These approaches to leading and organizing tended to emphasize productivity, output, and competency. They were sometimes effective in short-term experiments or projects but also contributed to a steady rise in stress, burnout, and the eroding of employee engagement in the long-term.

This notion that we can or should be professional in one context and personal in others is just not held up by research or lived experience. Instead, we find that when we experience empathy at work or school, we are better friends, partners, parents, and community members; and when we experience deeper care at home, we can be more resilient, even-tempered, and open-minded on the job.[57]

In fact, studies have shown that empathetic workplaces "tend to enjoy stronger collaboration, less stress, and greater morale, and their employees bounce back more quickly from difficult moments such as layoffs."[58] And yet the practice of empathy in the workplace remains rare, or at least unevenly distributed and unpredictably dependable.

The first principle of *the KOAN method* is to reclaim Kindness as a core cultural attribute across the spheres of our lives.

To create the conditions that foster connection and creativity and build the way to a common good, we've got to remember that we are human, first and always.

As we will explore, a Kind culture isn't necessarily a "nice" one and certainly isn't premised in any surface notions of politeness or civility that too often are the spit-polished window dressing for control and exclusion. Instead, the journey to Kind begins with empathy, is rooted in real curiosity, and is founded on a premise that we are more creative, receptive, and generative when we aren't afraid.

Fear—whether it is triggered by a physical or social threat—sends us into survival mode, activating the oldest parts of our brain and triggering the fight-flee-freeze-fawn responses that are hard-wired into our nervous system to protect us from harm. Dr. Bessel Van Der Kolk calls this the brain's "smoke detector."[59] While it is the reason our ancestors survived so that we could be born, and is still a big help if we're being chased down a dark alley or stalked by a wild animal, in the social contexts where we have to work with other (similarly wired) humans, the constant beep of that smoke detector makes it impossible for us to connect deeply with others or to access the creativity necessary to solve complicated problems. When we are in a survival state, the only question we can answer is "Am I safe?"

Cultivating Kind cultures requires that we develop the skills and tools to recognize when this survival response is being triggered (in ourselves and others) so that we can better recover our collective ability to connect (emotional state) and think, imagine, and create (executive state).

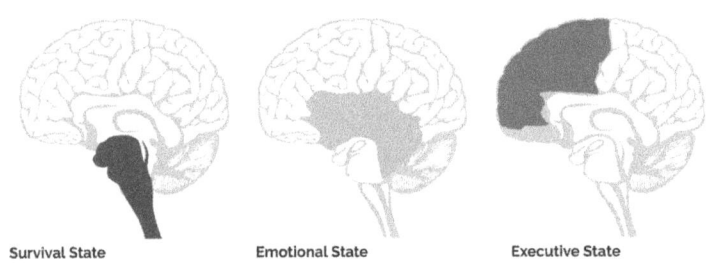

Survival State   Emotional State   Executive State

Figure 2: Conscious Discipline's Brain-State Model[60]

Being at our best more often and in more places is easier when we aren't always on edge, or wondering whether we are going to be rewarded or punished from moment to moment.

Far too many people routinely experience some form of bullying in the workplace.[61] This toxic behavior can manifest in all kinds of ways and produce different impacts and responses in different people; but when it becomes a consistent hallmark of an organization's culture, it can wreak havoc and interfere with getting good work done together.[62]

For lasting change to occur, interrupting these dynamics and building new habits has to happen at multiple levels of impact. To change things on a large scale, we must also be able to look in the mirror. Organizations, communities, and social systems are made up of people interacting with one another day in and day out. Transformation and healing begin with a spirit of care and a remembering that we need each other "close in."

As the poet David Whyte says:

> *Start close in,*
> *don't take the second step*
> *or the third,*
> *start with the first*
> *thing*
> *close in,*
> *the step*
> *you don't want to take.*

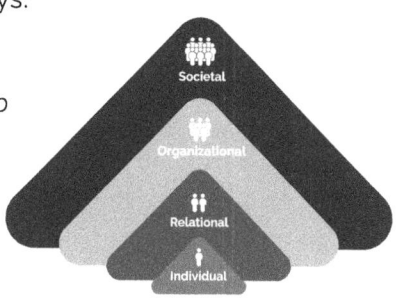

Figure 3. Levels of Impact

For most of us, that first step is the one that confronts what we've been missing and has us look ourselves in the eye.

Doing our own **individual** work (and admitting there are things we have yet to learn and that we have likely even caused harm because of ignorance or hubris) is where the journey begins. Only when we can feel love for ourselves can we extend that feeling to others. For most of us, this is the work of a lifetime! It is never over, nor is it ever too late to begin.

As we become more solid in our own skin (I always loved the French phrase *bien dans sa peau,* which translates literally to "good in their skin," to describe someone who is happy, fulfilled, and generally likes themselves), we find that we can show up differently in *relational* contexts. When we are less threatened, and therefore less defended and defensive, we can let our guard down, become more curious, listen more deeply, and connect in ways that can transform dynamics in all directions.

Before we can tend to transformation in groups (teams, communities, organizations) or in systems, we have to learn to cultivate containers of care close in with one another.

Creating Psychological Safety

As soon as people begin to emerge from their survival state, they want to know they are cared for. The old adage that people won't care how much you know until they know how much you care is borne out again and again in practice. One of the best reasons to build a Kind culture is that it helps people shift from worry and reactivity to inspiration and creativity. In 2012, Google launched Project Aristotle and spent two years studying what characteristics make a team successful. When they began, they had notions that selecting the smartest people, or the most experienced managers would make a successful team. What they discovered was that what really frees a team to shine is a context of psychological safety in which members are free (and encouraged) to ask hard questions and challenge and push the envelope of new ideas. At the end of the study, the findings were clear: "Teams with psychologically safe environments had employees who were less likely to leave, more likely to harness the power of diversity, and ultimately, who were more successful."[63]

Just as we began our learning journey with a HIKE, the CARE mantra gives us a helpful way of thinking about how to create an environment in which people feel enough safety to snap out of survival mode and access their ability to connect, reflect, and innovate.

Leaders create containers of CARE when they *Connect* purposefully with their teams, *Affirm* what they hear and validate others' experiences, *Regulate* their own emotional state (and can help others do so, too), and *Empower* those around them to try hard things and learn from the experience.

This is the container in which real innovation and creativity are born.

Creating an environment of psychological safety is not the same as policing speech or protecting feelings. Its purpose is to create environments where we can say the hard things that need to be said and explore difficult truths honestly, so our identities can be open to broader perspectives, experiences, or understandings.

The first step in cultivating this kind of environment is to **Connect**, on purpose and with intentionality. This begins with knowing who we are, how we are wired, and what we believe in strongly enough to allow ourselves to be known by others—and to care enough to learn other's stories, too. The saying that we must "put our own oxygen mask on first" applies to our leadership, too. This self-awareness allows us to care for our well-being and the impact we have on others (the leadership shadow we cast). This, in turn, helps us to cultivate a quality of relationship that allows others to be seen and feel known.

Cultivating connection requires an ability to stay with our own emotions—to not numb or avoid them but to move instead into full feeling. Recent research shows that most addictions (alcohol, drugs, food, technology, sex, shopping, etc.) stem not from a lack of willpower or some inherent biological predisposition but from a profound sense of disconnection—that the opposite of addiction is not sobriety, but connection.[64]

When we lean into relationship, we create a virtuous cycle that has a positive effect on our emotional state in the moment and fosters the conditions for thriving over time.

This depth of connection can feel very vulnerable, especially at first, and so, as leaders, partners, or guides, it's important that we **Affirm** others' experience. When our experience is invalidated, it can feel like a threat or violation that sends us right back into a survival state. When we feel seen and heard, our nervous system relaxes.

Leaders can counteract this by developing their skills in active listening, appreciative inquiry, and therapeutic techniques such as providing unconditional positive regard,[65] accepting and respecting people just as they are. This doesn't mean that anything goes but it does mean recognizing that negating people's identities or experiences does damage to the foundation of relationship that creates psychological safety and is an ineffective strategy for co-creative problem-solving.

When we experience validation, we experience a rush of "happy" hormones, like dopamine and oxytocin, which turns down our sympathetic nervous system (the fight-flight-freeze-fawn response) and activates a parasympathetic response (rest and digest). From this state we have more access to the tools that help us **Regulate** our emotional response. This can help us move out of a survival state and regain access to the thinking, reasoning, and creativity that is available from an executive state.

Leaders who are good at creating containers of care are wise to first learn their own triggers and the strategies that work best for self-recovery. This could be tuning into our breath, practicing mindfulness, using biofeedback strategies, naming what we are feeling, moving our bodies, spending time in nature, journaling, and so on. As we find the strategies that fit us best, we also learn how to help others access what works best for them, and how to weave access to those things into our environments.

Workplaces that keep people under chronic stress not only have higher levels of burnout and greater employee turnover, but they also feed toxic dynamics like gossip, cliques, and workplace bullying. Cultivating practices that restore system regulation can help us reengage our thinking brain and liberate creativity, confidence, and problem-solving.

Leaders who foster this feeling of competence **Empower** their teams as they begin to feel unstuck. When we can look at old challenges with new eyes, we are able to feel excited and energized by the different perspectives around us instead of being threatened by or defensive about them. The leader who can create this kind of container of care will help their team bring forward their best thinking.

In her book *Multipliers*,[66] Liz Wiseman highlights the strategies that leaders use to empower their teams and help unleash their full potential. These leaders are the opposite of "diminishers" who bully, belittle, and strong-arm their teams into compliance while building their own fiefdoms and organizational empires. Instead, "multipliers" offer encouragement, gather input, model making tough decisions, and truly trust their people to get great things done together.

CARE Mantra

When creativity is low and tensions are high, it is an indicator that a group or team is on edge. This mantra helps us explore strategies to shift from reactivity to creativity by creating the containers of CARE that support psychological safety.

Chapter Four—Cultivating Kind Cultures

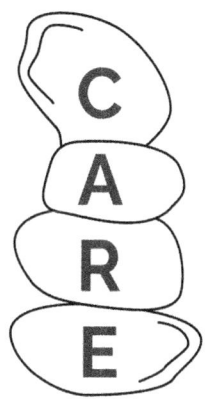

How can I foster deeper *CONNECTION*?

Are my interactions helping or hindering?

What needs *AFFIRMATION* here?

Who needs to feel seen or heard?

What will support physical and emotional *REGULATION*?

What support can I provide?

Where is *EMPOWERMENT* flourishing?

Where is it not? What is my role in fostering it?

Cultivating this type of trust can be challenging for leaders who are still early in their own learning journeys, but as we grow ourselves and begin to internalize more deeply that our leadership success comes from the strength of our teams and not from our own acumen or expertise, it gets easier to trust in trust as being the foundation of breakthrough leadership and to create meaningful containers of CARE for our teams.

For leaders and their teams, the antidote to a cultural context in which posturing and bravado have become a competitive sport lies in building new models that will make the old ones obsolete.

Cultivating Kind cultures is the first step into a beyond-bullying world.

Beyond Bullying

Turning on the TV or scrolling social media can sure make it look like whoever puffs up their chest the biggest and tears down their opponents most loudly gets the prize. But even when they do, it's not without great costs. And we get to decide if this is the world we want to build.

Early in human history, core survival needs often meant that being bigger and stronger was somewhat better. Whoever could get more (food, shelter, fire, resources, etc.) tended to win the day. Differences were viewed as threats to be avoided or killed off. Physical strength, brute force, or the ability to gather and hoard resources were often the key determinants of who had and could hold onto power.

Yet even these stories we've told ourselves for centuries about early human communities are partially incomplete. In their fascinating review of how history has come to be told, David Graeber and David Wengrow highlight how much more complex and nuanced the archeological evidence is, and who benefitted socially and politically from the story being told in this way. Deterministic descriptions of our ancestors as either simple and unsophisticated or savage and barbarian helped fuel imperial conquests, justified military and industrial expansion, and was often used to refute indigenous critiques of European methods and mores.[67]

In any case, these models of domination and control certainly don't serve us in a world where information about anything that anyone does flies across the globe in a nano-second, and where the choices a company or community makes on one side of the world can have ripple effects thousands of miles away. For most people most of the time, winner-takes-all models lead to disappointment and defeat. They also encourage winning by any means necessary, which fosters corruption and cheating and almost inevitably leads to an uneven playing field where winning odds are unevenly distributed.

Creating kind cultures is not about being nice; it is about fostering environments that favor flourishing over fear and creating the conditions for creativity that can unleash the kind of imagination necessary to solve any problem.

Being Kind means not asking employees to leave their hearts at home, and instead creating policies that are overtly, intentionally, and unapologetically heart-centered.

To help people shift out of survival mode, we first must create conditions of safety where norms and expectations are clear, bad surprises are rare, contributions are acknowledged and appreciated, and the tools and information necessary to make good decisions are in place. When people feel seen, respected, and trusted, they do great work.[68] Instead, we have too often built reward systems that don't serve a future most of us want to live in. We have prized competition over collaboration and created cultures of corruption and greed.

We have passed these models off as rational and market-driven, but we only have to look at the differences in pay between men and women, between diverse groups,[69] and at the massive difference in the way we compensate even the most essential[70] workers to see that the people who provide what we want and need most are not the people who are best paid, appreciated, or celebrated for their work.

We can resist the notion that kindness matters or that empathy belongs in the workplace, but the evidence overwhelmingly shows that when people are afraid for their health or security and are in survival mode, they think in narrow and short-term ways at the expense of mutually thriving futures.

But some change is beginning. ESG investing, which focuses on Environmental, Social, and Governance criteria, is growing; and not just because it is the kind, nice, or right thing to do but because the way we've been doing things for more than a century isn't sustainable. It is already reaching a breaking point, and ESG metrics help companies evaluate how well they are set up to adapt in a changing world and allow investors to see who is being proactive about planning for the long haul.

At the individual level, more and more organizations are recognizing that truly great performance comes from inspiration, not manipulation, and they are implementing ideas like minimum basic incomes and recognition systems that reward those who make things better for everyone instead of those who compete only for their own benefit.

Failing to change reward systems, whether in giant corporations or in how we pay teachers, nurses, and all manner of essential workers, dooms change efforts by incentivizing bullying behavior over creativity and common-good solutions.

Sometimes we need a little something to startle us out of complacency and to remind us that the way things are is at least partly a function of where we put our attention. Yes, power dynamics are almost always at play, but we have a part to play in the dance. One of the first steps in building a new model is believing that it can be done and that fantastic things are possible.

Chapter Four—Cultivating Kind Cultures

Poetic Pause
Fantastic Things

June 15, 2021

Life sometimes
Often, even
Surprises us
With its vagaries.

When we resign
Ourselves to
Solitude
Company arrives.

When we give up
On our dreams
They refuse
To give up on us.

When we determine
To accept
Whatever comes,
Abundance arrives at last.

If it strikes us as irony
That letting go
Draws us near
To our heart's desire,

We haven't been
Paying attention
To how
It all works.

the KOAN method

Fantastic things
Are drawn
To the
Fantastic.

Amazingly,
It is
Just
That simple.

When we allow,
Indulge,
Enjoy,
Our fantasies

They become
Manifest
In ways
We can't even imagine.

Only then,
Does the true
Test
Emerge.

Will we trust,
Have faith,
Believe
Enough

To give
The fantastic things
The room they need
To take root and blossom?

*Only then,
Will we learn
That we are already
Worthy.*

*And, here's the catch
Our joy
Magnifies
The joy of others.*

*Our love
Makes it possible for
Others to
Know love.*

*How easy it is
To lose sight
Of the truth
Of who we are.*

*But how important
It can be to
Take on faith
That miracles can happen.*

*How fantastic
Would it be
If we all just
Believed that, a little more . . .*

A KOAN Case Study: Radical Generosity in Action

In 2015, toward the end of my first cohort experience with my nature-based leadership group, I went on a solo overnight just outside of Crestone, Colorado. It was something of an initiation for me and I was nervous. I'd had my fifth knee surgery only six months earlier and was anxious about being alone in the wilderness. One of the magical things about cultivating communities of connection, though, is that we begin to learn that we can find support from many places and are never really alone. Without ever pushing, my sister-friends encouraged me to explore the experience that was being offered by the community and by the land itself.

It's funny to me now, but also a little poignant, to look back at how afraid I felt. While I wasn't ever going to be too far from the other women who were also solo, and we had a buddy system in place in case of emergency, I still felt unsettled as I set up camp. As dark descended, I spent several hours listening to the rustling of the tent and all manner of noises outside that made my heart skip and race. While camping wasn't new to me, I was feeling particularly vulnerable. Eventually, nature called, and I gathered the courage to poke my nose out into the darkness.

As I pulled myself out into the fall air and stood in a little clearing, I realized that the night sky was anything but dark. Bathed in moon and starlight, I felt connected to and supported by the universe in a way that felt both new and as old as time. Instantly, any feeling of separation or aloneness vanished, and I heard a voice in my heart clearly say, "Your people are out there; go and find them." I knew that these women with whom I'd climbed mountains, explored the desert, and walked beaches were just the beginning and that there were more of us out there, ready to build a better way and aware that we needed each other to do so.

A few weeks later, I sat in the ballroom of a big hotel in San Francisco, surrounded by more than 500 kindred spirits at an Emerging Women conference, listening to Vicki Saunders share devastating statistics about the amount of venture capital funding that goes to women entrepreneurs (less than 4% at the time and down to 2.3% by 2020).[71]

It was what she said next that jolted me awake, though. After having launched and exited several companies herself, and now with a front row seat to the investment scene, she was tired of tinkering around the edges and was out to build another way. Her recent book highlighted how "SheEOs" thought about and operated their businesses differently.[72] Founders and CEOs who identified as women, she said, operated less in isolation and more from a spirit of Radical Generosity and mutual care.

She was bringing that spirit to a new model of funding—inviting communities of women to contribute $1,000 each to a shared fund and then deciding together how to distribute those resources to support enterprises that were working on the world's most pressing problems. I got excited and got involved. First as an "Activator," contributing funds and participating in the venture selection and then as an early ambassador, supporting the expansion of the model from Canada to the U.S. in 2016.

Over the next seven years, SheEO would raise more than 15 million dollars of capital and distribute it in a regenerative cycle to more than 170 small businesses around the world. By starting from principles of connection and kindness, crucial funding flowed not only to leaders like Jane Chen, whose story we explored earlier, but to dozens of Ventures aimed at addressing the United Nations Sustainable Development Goals. Beyond the elegant simplicity of the economic model, the movement shows what is possible when we begin with empathy and trust in connection: we unleash the creativity necessary to solve big problems, together.

As the network of Activators and Ventures grew, connected, and shared insight, wisdom, support, and resources with one another, the model spread to Australia, New Zealand, and the UK, and the organization itself began to adapt and evolve. In 2022, the community renamed itself from SheEO (which focused on individual entrepreneurs) to Coralus (to reflect the collective community and its impacts) and ratified this credo:[73]

At the core of Coralus is the belief that practicing Radical Generosity creates a new and better world.

Here, we have all that we need to reach our potential.

If you need something, ask.

If you have something to give, please offer it.

We are all at different stages and ages and we come from different experiences.

We are here with our sleeves rolled up, ready to help one another.

This is a co-created environment built on trust.

We are creating a space for people to thrive on their own terms.

We take our time and we consider the future.

We celebrate and embolden each other.

We amplify each other's voices.

We own our greatness.

This community is debunking the notion that caring is at odds with business success and impact. In their 2021 Venture Impact Report,[74] they showed a community supporting one another to thrive while still in mid-pandemic. Despite supply chain disruptions, ventures were exporting their products to 67 countries around the world and were making a positive difference in 16 of the 17 UN Sustainable Development Goals.[75] Moreover, those ventures were not just surviving but thriving inside the container of care that the community was building. Ventures had experienced 432% revenue growth since starting with SheEO and were employing hundreds of people around the world.

Figure 4: United Nations' Sustainable Development Goals

According to the report's authors, "Receiving funding and resourcing on their own terms has allowed SheEO Ventures to consider purposeful growth in their businesses, powered by the radical generosity of this community." This spirit of radical generosity, exemplified in how women tend to run and organize their businesses, has become much more than a guiding principle. The Coralus community has turned it into a way of being, declaring:

Radical Generosity is a practice...

In contrast to conventional systems built on extraction and accumulation, we organize around the intent to *share resources toward their highest and best use*. We enact Radical Generosity for our *individual and collective healing* and transformation. We are Radically Generous when we operate outside the transactional mindset most of us inherited from power structures like patriarchy, colonialism, and capitalism.

When we create offerings for the common good *without expectation* of individual return, we share in unexpected and valuable dividends. We've seen this *magic* over and over. Coralus is engineered to hold space for gestures, projects, and experiments with Radical Generosity at the center.

Experiencing this magic up close, and watching its impacts unfold across great distances, has reinforced my belief in the power of *Kind Cultures* to unleash creativity and inspire progress in wildly diverse communities. When we bring this kind of empathy to our work, not because it is nice but because it is what works best to motivate and support groups of humans to be great together, we can accomplish incredible things.

Empathy Heals

We have explored how individual leaders can create containers of care that foster psychological safety and unleash potential of the people on their teams. Similar principles apply as organizations and communities tackle the deep change that promotes healing at system scale.

As we cultivate breakthrough leadership in a world scarred by division, it is helpful to remember that the kind of future we want to build requires us to heal the trauma that many of us have experienced inside systems and structures that have been profit-over-people-centered for a very long time. The toll that "extraction" of all kinds has taken on both people and the planet shouldn't be underestimated or too quickly dismissed. Living inside dehumanizing systems erodes people's ability to connect with and trust one another in the ways we have learned are important for co-creativity, but there is hope.

Nelson Mandela was born in 1918 into a royal family in the South African village of Mvezo, where his father served as Chief. Well-educated and politically active from a young age, Madiba (as Mandela was often called, a sign of respect for his Xhosa clan name) was already a member of the African National Congress when white Afrikaners came to power in 1948 and enforced apartheid, a formal policy of segregation that severely curtailed the rights of non-whites and forbade them from serving in government in order to reinforce the power of the minority-white National Party.

After more than a decade of protesting and fighting for reforms, Mandela was arrested in 1961 and sentenced to hard labor at the notoriously brutal Robben Island Prison. For the next 18 years, he was subjected to the harshest of conditions but remained the symbolic leader of the anti-apartheid movement. As his reputation grew, he was eventually moved to lower-security environments. In 1990, almost 30 years after Mandela was first arrested, F. W. de Klerk was elected president and ordered his release as a demonstration of his commitment to building a nonracist South Africa.

the KOAN method

Subsequent negotiations between the two men earned them the Nobel Peace Prize in 1993. The following year, Mandela was elected the first black president of South Africa, voted into office in the first multiracial elections ever held in a country born of a complex Indigenous and Colonial history. While some people wanted to see Mandela retaliate against the outgoing government, he instead created the Truth and Reconciliation Commission to "investigate human rights and political violations committed by both supporters and opponents of apartheid between 1960 and 1994 [and] also introduced numerous social and economic programs designed to improve the living standards of South Africa's black population."[76]

It wasn't a cure-all for the country's stresses, but it was deeply symbolic in the moment and, in the decades since, it has changed the ground on which its people try to build a better tomorrow. Entire professions have grown up around fostering restorative[77] and/or transformative[78] justice worldwide.

While restorative justice practices are sometimes used by law enforcement or other official entities like schools and cities, transformative justice is a political framework that begins from the premise that changing systems and societies requires a radical reimagining of how to be in relationship to one another, a framework that can be hard to fully explore from within existing institutions. Both restorative and transformative philosophies begin by acknowledging that what reduces violent division most is healing.

To move organizations, communities, and whole systems out of trauma and into healing, we've got to learn to care at scale.

Transforming Communities and Systems

While anyone who leads from anywhere can leverage the CARE mantra to cultivate environments that move people out of survival mode and into their most resourced and creative selves, those who are moving the needle on our biggest challenges and trying to lead transformation at scale must know how to help systems HEAL.

This means being able to connect with people at a level sufficient to acknowledge often messy, complicated, and even ugly truths about our history, without getting mired in them.

It requires us to affirm those lived experiences and work to have real empathy for the lasting effects of the past.

That means we need to always be actively cultivating the practices that allow us to be sufficiently resourced to think creatively together so that we can come up with meaningful, situation-specific solutions and take action.

Systems are designed to persist, and they tend to, even when their purpose no longer serves. In working to change things that have institutional weight, one of the paradoxes of empowerment is that it often requires some measure of individual leadership to take the first step.

Creating caring containers is important at any scale. There are no easy one-and-done formulas for system transformation, but cultivating a disposition toward healing can be helpful. This means acknowledging people's *History* and its impacts, cultivating real *Empathy* for that lived experience, examining what *Action* would be meaningful as a result, and exercising *Leadership* to overcome the inertia of the status quo.

History isn't always easy to look at. In a world where information was scarce, history tended to be told by the victors and was often rewritten as power and influence shifted. Today, information is everywhere and the tools we have for piecing together the past are beyond impressive, but most of what we find will challenge the narrative that many of us have held as truth.

Asking ourselves what stories have been told publicly about these events and who have been made the heroes and villains can help us to see how history shapes our sense of who we are and how we experience the world. If there are different versions of the story, it's worth asking what those versions have in common, where they might differ, and whom they benefit.

Our experience of a divided world is, in part, caused by trying to elevate any one of those stories to supremacy. Recognizing that we each have only a small piece of the puzzle, we can relax our identity defenses and allow connection with each other at a level sufficient to cultivate real empathy.

Empathy can arise when we are able to stay in the discomfort of not knowing and shift to inquiry, allowing us to learn things that challenge some portion of an idea we hold dear. If we think there is supposed to be a right way, and "our way" feels threatened, it is easy to become defensive and critical of other people's experiences.

Notice what there is to learn from those who have walked a different path. How does enlarging our understanding and making room for a bigger story make us feel? As leaders, how do we make space for grief or invite celebration? Can we sit with one another in feelings of sadness, anger, and joy?

When we see that our perspective is always partial, it becomes easier to affirm the lived experience of those whose journeys have been different from our own and discover valuable new actions to take.

Getting into *Action* looks and feels different from this place of connection and empathy. From here we can explore how to forge a future that is both aware of where we've been and rooted in commitments to building a better tomorrow.

In the face of new insight, or as potential solutions begin to emerge, it can be tempting to react impulsively, but the attention we've paid to history and the work we've done to cultivate empathy can help us avoid knee-jerk responses that might create new and unintended harms. This is where the ability to build caring containers for people of diverse backgrounds and experiences becomes critical as we consider whose voices ought to be included and whose experiences there are to learn from. Albert Einstein is widely quoted as having said that one can't solve problems with the same level of thinking that created them. It's at this inflection point where we get to choose connection over division.

The choice to implement quick-fix solutions almost always paves the road to division and discontent, as some interests "win" at the expense of others. The path to breakthrough, on the other hand, is best carved by leaders who are able to look at the landscape from all angles and who bring diverse viewpoints and perspectives together to co-create mutually-thriving futures. Asking ourselves how we can design our change in ways that model the future we aspire to build and what will keep us true to our commitments along the way, charts a course to real innovation.

Leadership can take many forms. Sometimes it means leading from the front, being bold, and setting direction. Sometimes it means being the one who can listen quietly, taking it all in, hearing possibilities in the gaps, and offering just the right question or observation to shift collective thinking. Sometimes it means being the first follower who motivates others to join a movement.[79]

At systems-scale, cultivating empowerment and building momentum in the direction of a different future requires leadership to overcome the inertia of systems whose very reason for being is to endure. And, in a world that is at once as distributed and as connected as ours, no one person can hold all the cards or have all the answers.

Asking ourselves where we can step forward, spend our capital, leverage what influence we have to move the needle and put a movement in motion, sometimes means examining what role we can play in setting others up for success.

HEAL Mantra

Organizations, systems, and communities have legacies that can keep us mired in old patterns. This mantra helps us explore the past with curiosity and care so that we can build a better tomorrow.

Chapter Four—Cultivating Kind Cultures

HISTORY - What paths have we walked (personally, organizationally) to arrive here?

Who has benefited? Who has been harmed? What more is there for me to learn? How can I connect?

EMPATHY - How can we cultivate caring curiosity in the face of stories and experiences different from our own?

Are there things we need to mourn or grieve? Are there things to celebrate? How can I affirm the collective experience?

ACTION - Knowing what we now know, what new steps can we see to take?

What meaningful actions can we take in service of a better tomorrow? How will we resource ourselves for the journey?

LEADERSHIP - What qualities will be needed to get us where we want to go?

What paths will this leader have walked? What resources or support will they need? How can I empower their contribution?

Leadership happens in community, and making good decisions together requires some level of shared insight. Looking at different stories from different angles and picking out the path to a common good is easier if we withhold less and have fewer secrets.

When more of us have access to shared information, we can more easily make sense of it together.

That's why the next element of **the KOAN method** is fostering **Open Systems**.

Chapter Five

Fostering Open Systems

There are two mistakes one can make along the road to truth. Not going all the way, and not starting.

~ Seth Godin

When complex problems require co-creative problem-solving, shared access to relevant information becomes a crucial ingredient to building trust and liberating creativity. Yet many organizations are still built on secrecy and go to great lengths to restrict access to information. The systems built on secrecy are largely premised on principles that were intended for a time when it was hard to share the information and context necessary to interpret and make sense of data. Where they once served to maintain power and control over vast distances, today they impose those same strictures on systems that could operate instead with greater autonomy and fluidity in a more dynamic and interconnected way.

All sorts of military systems are built on keeping secrets. Things that might otherwise help friends and neighbors flourish are kept hidden for fear that enemies might exploit the information. Pharmaceutical companies can "protect" the formula for life-saving treatments (like the EpiPen or insulin) in ways that maximize their profits, leading to access for fewer people and exacerbating health and wealth disparities.

Compensation schemes have historically been kept private to bolster the negotiating position of the hiring employer over the prospective employee, while fostering cultural norms that make talking openly about salaries taboo. All manner of proprietary technology serves to consolidate and enrich corporate monopolies while making compatibility and interoperability a nightmare for consumers and limiting co-creative potential.

These habits of withholding critical information have become hardwired into much of modern life in ways that often disempower and constrain creativity.

Can you think of a time when you had to make a decision without having all of the information that would have been helpful to you? Did you ever choose to not share data that could have helped someone else make a better decision? Did you ever discover something after the fact that would have altered your perspective had you known sooner? Has anyone ever found out that you kept something from them? What effect did these concealments have on trust and relationships?

We tend to think that there is a competitive advantage to withholding information, but that is only true if we subscribe to a win-lose scarcity model.

Ultimately, secrecy serves to divide and separate, instilling a sense of superiority for those in the know and spawning elaborate schemes to restrict the free flow of information. Ultimately, the drive to be superior builds a world where we are either scrambling to be on top or working to hold on to that position.

These secrecy moves are inherently separation moves and reinforce a false belief that we can build a good life in a world of winners and losers. We create a model where being better-than requires that others fill a less-than role, and the stress of being one or the other grows increasingly. In a world where access to information is more ubiquitous, the more we try to hide, the more we invite scrutiny and sow distrust.

The second principle of **the KOAN method** is to foster **Openness**, not only by sharing more information in a broader way, but by creating conditions for voices to be heard and by cultivating the capacity to be affected by new ideas and perspectives. Doing this is made easier by shifting our focus from what might appear to be short-term individual gains inside a toxic system to building common good solutions that make the whole system healthier.

There is a vast amount of research that shows that operational transparency increases trust[80] with both customers and employees. When people understand how things work or how decisions are made, they have greater faith in systems than when information is kept behind the curtain.

Yet, transparency and privacy also operate in a delicate dance with one another, especially in environments where power is unevenly distributed.

Absent a strong foundation of relationship, expectations that everything happens out in the open may foster inhibitions and lead to increased conformity as people strive to fit in[81] or seek approval. It is easier to share information and be open to its influence inside a container of care where trusting relationships are actively being cultivated. Finding the sweet spot where people can access the information that they need to do their job and make decisions, while allowing for that same information to be viewed by different people with different perspectives, is a critical ingredient in unleashing innovation and fostering breakthrough solutions.

In this section, we'll explore what becomes possible when we spend less time trying to get a leg up in a contest where the game is rigged and, instead, focus on rewriting the rules so that more of us are consistently thriving.

Coming up with solutions like that may require coming down from one's pedestal and looking each other in the eye, but we might also find that we can get even better outcomes than expected when we aren't looking over our shoulder or plotting our next move.

Harnessing the power of openness requires giving more people access to relevant information that can fuel breakthrough insights and foster the conditions that allow those ideas to come forward and influence decision-making.

Breakthrough leaders cultivate the trust required to do this well.

Leaders build trust when they are transparent with their teams, give them the information they need to contribute meaningfully, and then listen to their ideas. In *Radical Candor*,[82] Kim Scott lays out a management philosophy premised on caring personally (cultivating Kind cultures) while also challenging directly (which fosters Open systems). Habits of withholding, she suggests, have created toxic cultures in which we no longer know how to lovingly tell each other the truth.

So instead, we fall into habits of:

- *Ruinous Empathy:* where we smile, nod, and "be nice" to one another's faces, but complain and criticize behind each other's backs in ways that erode relationship, community, and trust;

- *Manipulative Insincerity:* where we say what we believe someone wants to hear in order to avoid difficulty or get what we want without really meaning it; or

- *Obnoxious Aggression:* where we bully, criticize, or dominate our way to achieving compliance or acquiescence but fall far short of true commitment.

These moves erode trust and create a vicious cycle where the more we withhold, the less we are trusted; and the less we share, the lower our faith is in those around us. The toxic cultures these behaviors create drive the truth underground and create enormous risk in systems because people will either not speak up, will not be heard, or will not be believed if they do voice themselves.

Many leadership scholars have developed models for building trust. Below, I highlight two and offer an easy way to remember the tenets they have in common.

Building a Strong Foundation

Getting great work done together and freeing breakthrough thinking requires a foundation of trust that enables and empowers individuals to bring their best thinking forward in service of the whole. This is supported by cultivating containers of care in the ways we explored in the last chapter and reinforced by behaviors that instill confidence and build credibility. While cultivating Kind cultures creates the conditions in which bravery can occur, fostering truly Open systems requires a foundation of trust sufficient to team members taking personal risks to build common good solutions.

While there are literally dozens of models, frameworks, and descriptions describing how to cultivate trust in teams, I have often turned to those developed by Brené Brown in *Dare to Lead*[83] and by Steven M. R. Covey in *The Speed of Trust*.[84] Looking at their frameworks side by side reveals some consistent principles to live and lead by.

There is plenty to like about both frameworks that, at their core, boil down to a few key principles to live by to foster trust.

Chapter Five—Fostering Open Systems

Brené Brown's BRAVING Framework	Steven Covey's Speed of Trust Principles
1. **Boundaries** Set clear expectations about what is ok or not, and why	1. **Extend Trust** Assess risk, then let go with confidence; empower your team
2. **Reliability** Be true to your word; keep commitments; don't overpromise	2. **Behave Your Way to Credibility** Walk your talk; actions speak louder than words
3. **Accountability** Own mistakes; don't deflect; apologize and make it right	3. **Make it Safe to Tell the Truth** Invite feedback without reprisal; demonstrate receptivity
4. **Vault** Respect people's stories; don't share what isn't yours	4. **Right Wrongs** We all make mistakes; own yours, and make amends
5. **Integrity** Be brave; do what's right; live your values in action	5. **Wear Glasses That Work** Confront reality; surround yourself with people who will tell the truth
6. **Nonjudgment** Ask for what you need, and honor others' needs w/o judging	6. **Talk Straight** Be honest and direct; share the whole truth if you are able
7. **Generosity** Assume positive intent; trust in people's common humanity	7. **Show Loyalty** Give credit to others where it is due and stand up for the absent

TRUST Mantra

When secrecy and withholding are present, leaders risk not receiving critical information in a timely way. This mantra helps us identify where breakdowns may exist and build foundations of mutual trust and transparency.

Chapter Five—Fostering Open Systems

TELL the truth

What can you share?
When privacy is required,
can you offer explanations
or provide helpful context?

RESPECT everyone

Are you treating all perspectives
as valid and all people
with dignity? How do you
demonstrate this?

UNDERSTAND yourself

Do you know your triggers?
What helps you recognize
your biases? How do you
live your values?

SHOW up

Do people expect you to follow
through and be dependable?
Does your intent match
your impact?

TAKE responsibility

When you make a mistake,
do you own it and make it right?
Where can you take
100% responsibility?

Chapter Five—Fostering Open Systems

Why, then, are these practices still so uncommon?

Understanding how and why we've built secrecy into systems can help us see where it no longer serves us and offer insights into how we can build new models.

Systems Built on Secrets

A lot of time, energy, and money go into preserving privacy and protecting the intellectual property and trade secrets that are the bread and butter of our economy today. And while some great ideas certainly deserve to be recognized and rewarded, most of the time secrets serve those who can afford to own and keep them.

During the rise of the industrial revolution, the ability to control knowledge, insight, and strategy became more important to organizational success than brute force alone. Making better tools, thinking creatively, and sharing knowledge consolidated power. This helped people, organizations, and nations control access to resources. It also gave the upper hand to the lawyers, politicians, and industrial titans who could write the laws, policies, and regulations that favored their ownership of patents, trade routes, and the means of production.

In a world where the opportunity to gain access to information varied widely, power was concentrated among those who had access to and could make sense of it.

While we've made a great deal of progress in the last century to reduce poverty and hunger and we've doubled the average life expectancy, we've also built a world where more people are deeply dependent on systems well outside of their control. Today, fewer people than ever know how to grow their own food, birth their own babies, tend to the sick, make their own clothes, or build their own homes.

Ultimately, this drive to keep and protect "secrets" creates division and builds a world where we are either scrambling to be in the know or working to keep what we know away from others.

Being Open means sharing as much information as you can, then sharing a little more. Far fewer things need to be kept secret or private than we might think; and transparency can be turned into a competitive advantage. When people have access to both information and insights, they make decisions and contribute from a place of genuine commitment rather from just punching a clock or ticking a box.

This multiplies the brainpower working to solve your organization or community's most important problems and increases the speed at which they can be solved.

Creating an environment of mutual trust opens people up to wanting to do their best work and gives them the tools to do so.

Too often, we are asked to trust that the "right" and "smart" people have thoroughly reviewed and impartially weighed the available evidence and come up with decisions in the best interest of the collective. We know, though, that these data sets are also historical products filled with assumptions, values, and presumptions that are meant to favor the few over the many.

Whenever we advance solutions that perpetuate or worsen inequities, we are just building a more inequitable world—and we all suffer the consequences of that. The way out of this vicious cycle is to shift our focus, from what might appear to be short-term individual gains inside a toxic system to building common-good solutions that make the whole system healthier.

Newer models like open-source software,[85] open-access data,[86] and open-book accounting[87] are creating alternatives that promote greater transparency. The Open University[88] and other online learning platforms are making traditional models of elite higher education less competitive and less desirable. More laws are being passed that require companies to publish salaries when hiring for a job, so that every applicant has a fair shot at being paid fair value for their work.[89] Corporate and public transparency regulations make it easier than ever to find out what the most senior leaders earn in organizations making the biggest impact on the communities around them.

Within organizations, leaders are recognizing that the biggest decisions they must make can't be made by a small group meeting behind closed doors—the data sets are too big, and the implications can best be interpreted by those closer to the work, not just those at the top.

When we foster open systems over closed ones, people have access to the information that most affects them, can make wiser decisions, and are able to think longer term about the impacts and implications of their actions. When we do this inside of cultures that are also kind, people feel empowered to use the information at their disposal and trusted to work for the common good.

This unleashes the true power of diversity in systems and enables a broader range of voices, representing differing vantage points, to inform, influence, and meaningfully shape new futures in ways that produce genuine breakthroughs.

This combination of Kind cultures and Open access to relevant information becomes rocket fuel for creativity, innovation, and breakthrough results; allowing us to chart new territory in conversation with one another and to discover possibilities we might never have dreamt up alone.

Chapter Five—Fostering Open Systems

Poetic Pause
Conversational Cartography
November 11, 2020

Sometimes, as we traverse the terrain of our lives,
It seems fitting to go it alone.
After all there is so often misunderstanding;
Lack of connection.

What seems so clear from where we stand,
Appears to elude others despite what so obviously sits
    before them.
So, we feel our way in the dark;
Grasping. Searching.

As we wander in this way, it can be hard to tell where the
    boundaries are;
To know where to start or stop,
When to backtrack
Or soldier on.

Here is the thing . . .
In wandering onward in this way
We learn less and less about ourselves and our journey;
Trapped by the chorus in our own minds.

As it happens, knowing ourselves happens only,
Really, in conversation.
It is how we make sense of things.
When Kenneth Burke said that we are:

"The symbol-using animal
Inventor of the negative . . .
Separated from [our] natural condition by instruments of
    our own making
Goaded by the spirit of hierarchy and rotten with perfection."

*He was daring us to recognize the ways that our words
Both create and confuse;
Clarify and conflate
Inquiry with insight.*

*We like to put things in tidy order.
We ascribe sense to the non-sensical.
Sometimes, we do the opposite too.
We doubt that which might make sense from another
    vantage point.*

*This is where conversation comes in.
It heightens our senses;
Fosters echolocation . . .
Broadens our perspective and, therefore, territory.*

*You see, when we send out the sensemaking we are doing,
And get back the seeing others have of us,
We are confronted
With the paradox of ourselves.*

*We discover that how we live in our own minds
Is often, mostly even, at odds with our occurrence in the
    world at-large.
This can be especially painful when those whose reflection
    matters most is in tension
With how we want ourselves to be known and seen.*

*Is this because they so want us to be like them that they
    cannot see us as we are,
Or because, knowing us so well they see us more clearly
    than we ever could?
What matters most, I think, is how we receive the gift that
    is returned
When we send these signals out into the world.*

When we encounter a mirror that is not to our liking,
Or challenges our sense of who we are,
Or want so very desperately to be,
Do we open up, or shut down?

Do we turn our tender underbelly
Toward the one who inquires
And lean into vulnerable revelation
Or cloak ourselves in the armor of defensive explanation?

The trouble, as I see it, is that when we pull back far enough
We are left only with our own internal critics and adoring fans
To calibrate our sensibilities.
We circle the same territory; gathering evidence.

This sometimes feels safe, or even affirming,
But is also hard and can be lonely.
The trickster in our inner world
Is cunning.

In doing the thing we hope will set us
Free from the judgments of others,
We cloister ourselves off from all
That vulnerable connection might unlock.

One can spend entire lifetimes
In this dance of sending out and receiving back
Without ever allowing ourselves to be affected, moved,
  changed;
And so, we find ourselves again, always, in the same story.

The mapmaker knows, though, that to
Plot a territory well,
One must examine it
From many angles.

the KOAN method

There is no single instrument,
Nor straight line,
That will yield a reliable
Charting of the terrain.

One might, perhaps,
Construct something
Adequate for retracing
One's own steps,

But no one else will ever be able
To use the artifact of that expedition
To find
Their own way.

In conversation, though
Every episteme is put at risk
And therefore, made both more robust
And more nuanced, at once.

Truly open inquiry leads to insight.
Each new flash of awareness
Yields new avenues of inquiry.
In opening to another, we find ourselves anew.

There is magnificence in this unfolding
If we allow it to grow our capacities and faculties
Not just for telling the story of ourselves,
But for loving that terrain from every angle.

Perhaps that is the point after all.
Maybe there is no
Perfectly accurate map to be made.
There is just the one that gets us where we want to go.

Chapter Five—Fostering Open Systems

A KOAN Case Study: Open IDEO

IDEO was founded in the 1990s by David Kelley, a pioneer of the process we now call Human-Centered Design—a true customer or user-first approach, rooted in empathy and bolstered by a willingness to prototype and iterate a LOT. This approach creates optimal conditions for contrasts to emerge as we see what does and doesn't get us where we want to go.

IDEO's Creative Difference model has helped to spur the development of innovative products like wearable breast pumps, vertical farming, pharmaceutical pill packs, and even a smart jacket[90] developed collaboratively with Levi's and Google to help both cyclists and truckers access common technology needs while minimizing device use on city streets and open highways.

This product is a great example of companies getting beyond rigidly guarded trade secrets and intellectual property to co-create a product that solves a problem. Recognizing the need for people in motion to safely access and navigate information technology, the two iconic brands teamed up with IDEO to design a jacket that was fashionable, comfortable, and practical and that seamlessly integrated gesture and touch to control key device functions.

Originally born out of the same tenets on which the Stanford Design (d.) School was built, IDEO had a front row seat to the magic that comes from co-creative imagination as they helped organizations ideate, prototype, and iterate their way to one innovation after another.

Over time, they also began to apply those principles to themselves, using design-thinking strategies to forge partnerships with "hotels, food banks, foundations, and entrepreneurs to combat food waste."[91] At its core, design-thinking fosters open exploration and both the Food Waste Challenge, and the Food Waste Alliance that it spawned, has helped to reduce the billions of tons of food wasted every year.

Now, the Open IDEO platform allows people from all around the world to collaborate to solve some of our stickiest challenges. From curing cancer to solving food insecurity—varied ideas lead to better solutions. The Open IDEO platform makes it easier for more people to lend their creative thinking to the problems most in need of innovation.

The Open Innovation model on which the platform is built begins from the belief that "to solve today's complex problems, there need to be better ways to come together, share ideas, and coordinate action around the globe . . . [this model helps] people worldwide break barriers, find support, and iterate on the ideas of many to create real change."[92]

The challenges this open-to-the-global-public environment is set up to solve are not issues that can be addressed inside the walls of any one organization or remedied by a single country's government policies or interventions. Systemic problems like improving childhood immunization, promoting menstrual health around the world, or decreasing global food waste need to be anchored in the best scientific data and tailored to the unique cultural, geographic, and geopolitical circumstances of local communities.

In 2019, Open IDEO and the Bill and Melinda Gates Foundation teamed up with more than 18,000 changemakers from more than 128 countries to answer the question, "How might we empower caregivers to seek and fully utilize immunization services in their communities?" The solutions proposed resulted in accelerator funding being delivered to 31 prototype programs that coordinated the services of 3,450 caregivers all around the globe.

Having launched just before the start of the COVID-19 pandemic, the newly established networks of connection and communities of support allowed these programs to pivot quickly and leverage existing relationships and resources to advance preexisting goals, while also tailoring and adapting them to the massive changes and health impacts caused by the pandemic.[93]

Principles of Open access and co-creative idea generation also influence how education is delivered and how educators engage, adapt, and co-create their lessons to support and serve diverse student populations.

The principle of Open Education is rooted in commitments to high-quality education as a human right and founded on the belief that empowering learners to understand the roots of ideas allows them to be more actively engaged in their own learning and development.[94]

When education is determined, defined, and controlled by a small number of already influential people, it tends to serve as a tool of indoctrination that can actively work against creativity and innovative thinking.

By leveraging publicly available resources and making transparent where those ideas are sourced, Open Education supports both educators and learners in having greater agency over their sensemaking.

By situating the educational experience in a historical, cultural, and political context that makes underlying value systems more explicit, they become more available to inquiry, critique, and co-creative evolution.

Open = Receptive

Closed systems pose challenges not only when they aren't transparent but also when they aren't receptive. When we don't extend trust to others with what we share, we also tend to not trust what they tell us, or we find it not important to listen. Confirmation bias occurs when we go in search of ideas that support, affirm, or reinforce what we already believe at the expense of perspectives that might challenge our understanding.

Time and again after major disasters, the after-action reports find a core reason for things going wrong being directly tied to crucial information not getting to the people who needed it or to decision-makers ignoring important input.

I was in middle school and living in France in 1986 when the Space Shuttle Challenger was scheduled to launch its first civilian crew member, schoolteacher Christa McAuliffe, into space. As was common in European schools at the time, I was home over a long midday break and helping to make lunch in the kitchen with my mother. The TV was on in the other room, and I remember repeatedly checking to see if the countdown to takeoff had begun. Finally, it did. I watched, first in excitement and delight as the rockets fired and liftoff began, and then in horror, seconds later, as a giant puff of white smoke and falling debris filled the screen. The voices of the commentators made clear that this was not how things were meant to go.

Chapter Five—Fostering Open Systems

The Rogers Commission[95] report, which details the cause of the accident, includes dozens of pages analyzing the technical failures that caused the explosion—feature flaws that allowed gasses to leak in extremely cold weather and combust as they came in contact with the heat from the rockets. These scientific findings ultimately conclude that "the cause of the Challenger accident was the failure of the pressure seal in the aft field joint of the right Solid Rocket Motor. The failure was due to a faulty design unacceptably sensitive to a number of factors."

While these technical reasons explain how and why the *explosion* occurred, the *accident* was ultimately caused by a failure in decision-making, and the report concludes that "the decision to launch the Challenger was flawed," based on testimony that revealed:

"Failures in communication resulted in a decision to launch [shuttle flight] 51-L based on incomplete and sometimes misleading information, a conflict between engineering data and management judgments, and a NASA management structure that permitted internal flight safety problems to bypass key Shuttle managers."

In particular, the report highlights how the concerns of "Level III NASA personnel and element contractors" regarding the resilience of the Solid Rocket Motor joint seal to extreme cold, and prior erosion of those seals from prior mission flights, were not adequately communicated to, or acted upon, by "Level I and II" NASA leaders responsible for making launch decisions.

Fostering the kind of trust that promotes open sharing well before a crisis looms means getting information into the right people's hands when it is needed most and ensuring that the conditions exist for it to be heard, made sense of, and acted upon. Not surprisingly, many other accidents have resulted from failures in communication:

Design flaws in the Chernobyl nuclear reactor resulted in disaster,[96] but the fact that the operators were unaware of those flaws or of prior accidents left them unprepared to prevent or respond to the disaster as it began to unfold.

On September 11, 2001, the planes that crashed into the World Trade Center the Pentagon, and into a Pennsylvania field, killed hundreds of people. But failures in communication technology and in poor or nonexistent habits of communication and coordination between first-responder agencies[97] have been shown to have also contributed significantly to an increased death toll, including the loss of more than 300 firefighters who did not receive the same updates as their police counterparts during the evacuation of the towers.

Yet, four years later, many of these issues had still not been addressed or adequately resolved when Hurricane Katrina made landfall in New Orleans, Louisiana. Once again, technical and infrastructure failures were exacerbated by poor communication and disorganized leadership.[98,99]

When British Petroleum (BP) suffered a catastrophic failure of their Deepwater Horizon oil platform in 2010, the disaster claimed the lives of 11 people, spilled more than five million gallons of oil into the Gulf of Mexico, and created massive economic disruption in the region. The final report[100] found that human failures in leadership and communication got in the way of a rapid and appropriate response.

Time and again we find that, when information is withheld or ignored at critical moments, what might have remained a controlled technical problem, with a workable solution, can rapidly become a disaster with disproportionate human impacts. To transform closed systems into open ones, leaders can help to create environments where members feel safe and trusted; environments where members can share relevant information and share WHY that information is important.

When people are connected to a larger purpose, their sense of contribution not only increases, but their capacity to make sense of data and make insightful decisions that serve and support a shared direction increases.

As Simon Sinek has said, "We are drawn to leaders and organizations that are good at communicating what they believe. Their ability to make us feel like we belong, to make us feel special, safe, and not alone is part of what gives them the ability to inspire us."[101] Leaders who do this well help their teams articulate a clear vision and chart a viable way there.

Setting Inspired Direction

I've been involved in dozens of strategy-setting and planning efforts over the years and have found three persistent challenges: aiming high enough to be inspiring without getting mired in the details; getting concrete enough for the plan to feel actionable; and designing something that will cope with dynamic changes in the environment. The best plans set a bold goal that is deeply tied to organizational values and commitments; define a meaningful set of milestones and activities; and then thoughtfully confront what might get in the way, how the people and system will need to evolve to "get there," and how progress will be tracked so that course corrections are obvious and natural along the way.

When leaders engage all these items well, they inspire progress and help their teams chart a VIABLE Strategy™; because people have helped to shape the direction and are excited about where they are going and because the plan is practical and tangible enough for them to know where to start and how to adapt along the way.

This model has proven powerful for planning and implementing breakthrough projects, and it is also a helpful barometer of progress, allowing leaders and their teams to assess strengths and challenges, identify areas of opportunity, and adjust in the direction of shared goals. It becomes a helpful "scorecard" of sorts.

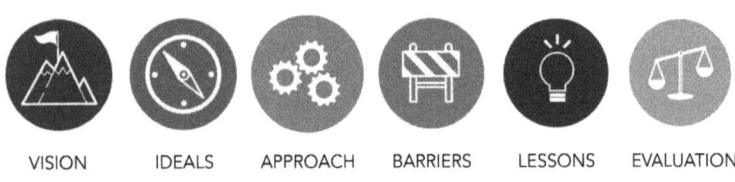

Figure 5: Integrated Work's VIABLE Strategy Model

Below we'll examine how defining a *Vision*, articulating *Ideals*, and crafting an *Approach* can help to foster **Open Systems**; and later we'll explore the other VIABLE elements as tools that enable and support us in **Being Adaptive**.

Setting a clear and compelling VISION. A leader's job in the face of any change, whether planned or unplanned, is to work with their team to set a star to steer by—this helps provide clarity in the face of uncertainty and reassures people that there is some overarching direction. The purpose of setting a clear vision is to articulate a bold trajectory for the duration of the plan, one that can inspire and motivate team members to chart their way there. This serves open systems by inviting courage and commitment over mere compliance. As Audre Lorde said, "When I dare to be powerful—to use my strength in the service of my vision—then it becomes less and less important whether I am afraid."[102]

Engaging a group in setting a clear and compelling vision moves them out of fearful day-to-day reactivity and connects them with a larger purpose that emboldens innovation.

Different organizations, systems, or communities may have different time horizons for their plans but, generally speaking, 3-5 years is a helpful timeline—far enough out to invite creativity and aspirational thinking, but not so far that things become overly hypothetical. To get there, it is helpful to look back and reflect on what has happened in the recent past. What did the world look like five years ago? What has come to pass that we were predicting then? What was not on our radar that caused disruption? Could any of those things have been better predicted? Then, looking ahead, explore what may happen in the world and what effects those changes are likely to have. What is exciting about those potential futures? What is daunting?

Now, articulate how your organization or community will position itself in the face of those dynamic possibilities. Brainstorm key words or phrases that capture the impact you want to have, the difference you believe you are well-suited to make, and the progress you want to achieve. Paint a vivid picture of what success will look like and work with your team to articulate what it will feel like to arrive at your destination and accomplish your goals. Then, tap the talents of the wordsmiths in your group to craft a coherent statement that pulls the key elements together in an exciting and easy-to-remember way. Ultimately it should be a useful guidepost for the team to steer by.

As we emerged from the pandemic, the team at Integrated Work began to craft a **Vision**. We began by imagining what it would look and feel like to live in the future we wanted to be a part of shaping. We knew that we wanted to have a hand in bringing a new way of leading and organizing into being, and we captured and refined our commitments like this:

> We are catalysts for creating a more Just world.

> We serve as an innovation hub for ourselves and the human systems we partner with to build a resilient, flourishing future.

Articulating IDEALS that will inform choices and guide behavior. With an aspirational direction clearly articulated, it is helpful to explore what principles, values, or **Ideals** will support you along the way. These may or may not be identical to your overall organizational values and should be as much a reflection of who you aspire to be or of how you will need to "show up" to reach your vision.

I like the word *ideals* because it implies a stretch and acknowledges that we may not yet be all the way there. Defining ideals begins with asking questions like "Who are we in the world?" "Who do we aspire to be?" "What keeps us going?" "What gives meaning to our work?"

What is valuable about articulating these ideals alongside your vision is their power to reinforce commitments, establish norms, and deepen trust. When a group of people gets clear on where they are going AND commits to showing up with, and for, one another in a particular way, it creates the conditions for true co-creativity.

A few years back, the board of a large, statewide health care organization we worked with defined their ideals like this:

> **Unity**—*We are a richly diverse state, and we serve vastly different communities. Unity does not mean uniformity but means we know that we are stronger together.*

> **Integrity**—*Our patients' faith in us is paramount. Building trust is critical to our ability to deliver excellent care and we operate with integrity, always, in all things.*

> **Collaboration**—*None of us can reach our goals in isolation. Getting where we are headed demands that we do the hard work of working through our differences.*

> **Love**—*We do this work because it matters. We operate from a place of loving care for our patients, the communities we serve, and one another.*

Groups can get impatient early in the process of ideal development. They want to jump straight from where they are going (vision) to what they will do to get there (approach). This leapfrogs the important question of how they want to show up along the way and what they will steer true to.

Inevitably, the conversations they end up having about what is important about the journey turn out to be some of the most potent, bonding, and transformational conversations, even if the group didn't want to have them at the outset. If you are in search of a breakthrough, don't skip this step.

The work that happens in these conversations has the power to create containers of care and to deepen trust in ways that ultimately have a meaningful effect on the solutions they generate and the path they forge toward the future.

Defining an APPROACH that is clear and broadly understood. I like to think of this work in terms of developing an approach instead of building a plan because the dynamic world we live in lends itself less to step-by-step progress and more to identifying milestones and waypoints on the journey. This activity is meant to answer the question "How will we get there?" and can be approached either topically or chronologically. You might find that your vision has several components and that organizing your work into themes or clusters of activity is helpful. Or there might be key time horizons that are important and things that must happen first before the next things become possible.

Whatever approach you take, the goal of this activity is to drive alignment on the types of effort and the categories of work required to move you in the direction of your vision. This is the time to sift through personal preferences and pet projects or identify non-starters that evoke strong objections or lack the breadth of support

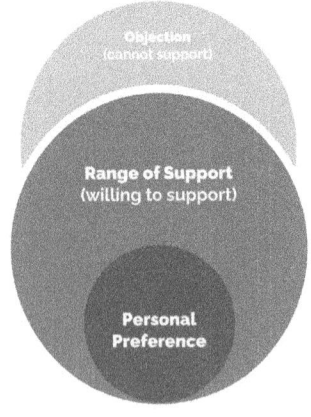

Figure 6: Range of Decision Support

to move forward. This will help you land on a range of solutions that individuals can champion and support.

You might think of this as a sensing activity that, given your vision, allows you to answer what you value, who you are in the world, and what your community needs from you. What key areas of strategic focus are most aligned with that vision?

Framing this as an approach instead of a plan allows for both focus and flexibility as you iterate your way to a desired future.

Doing this well allows team members to take ownership for individual activities and to understand how they fit in the context of the whole. If you have already cultivated a learning mindset, built containers of care, examined and addressed where your system might have healing work to do, and established a foundation of trust, you will find that team members are well positioned to ask for the information they need to help the whole system get where it wants to go and to raise issues and concerns when challenges arise (and before they become crises).

VIA(BLE) Mantra

Having a clear direction and shared commitments inspires groups of people to co-create exciting new futures. This mantra helps us set a course together and define how we want to show up on the way and sets key milestones for progress.

Chapter Five—Fostering Open Systems

Is your *VISION* clear and compelling?

Does your team know where they are headed, and are they inspired to get there?

Have you articulated *IDEALS* that will inform choices and guide behavior?

Are you clear about how you want to show up and how your behaviors will influence outcomes?

Do you have an *APPROACH* that is well-defined and broadly understood?

What milestones will serve as guideposts and help you stay the course in dynamic conditions?

We'll explore the second half of this model in the next chapter as we take a closer look at how to **Be Adaptive** as we explore how to build resilient learning systems that are able to shift and change with agility in the face of dynamic circumstances.

Chapter Six

Being Adaptive

Transformation is not accomplished by tentative wading at the edge.

~ Robin Wall Kimmerer

When was the last time you went to the doctor, planned a trip, tried to get a license, made a change to an official document, or attempted to get a refund on something and had a frictionless, joy-giving experience? If that's happened to you recently, the product or service provider can probably count on your loyalty for a long, long time.

Far too often, our experiences are the opposite of this—complicated, arduous, and time-consuming. If you don't have the kind of job that allows you to make hours-long calls during regular business hours or an education that has prepared you to read the convoluted details of fine print legal agreements, or you haven't been socialized to trust that policies and systems were designed for your benefit, you may have given up on being treated fairly by these systems or just opted out of them entirely whenever possible.

While policies and procedures can be helpful in scaling solutions, they only work if you can anticipate the full range of potential problems that might arise and expect that they won't change much over time. When conditions are more fluid, they can feed decision-paralysis as people fear stepping out of line or sticking their neck out. In a dynamic world, when both the challenges and their potential solutions shift and change much faster than any good policy manual can keep up with, it's much more effective to have a clear direction and guidelines that allow people who are close to the work to make smart choices in the face of dynamic conditions.

The third KOAN method principle is to **Be Adaptive**, which means fostering and encouraging flexibility and operating from principles rather than policies. When people can see how their contributions connect to the mission, they are better able to prioritize, shift gears, and evolve what they spend their time on to reach a desired shared result.

People who are empowered to identify, understand, and adapt to changes, and who are motivated and inspired to do so, will be able to solve more complex challenges in a dynamic environment. If the goal is to get somewhere together, this also means getting great at listening to the people who will be affected by our actions, inviting feedback, and bringing key stakeholders along.

The degree to which we have built containers of care and foundations of trust will play a big part in how empowered we can make a system and how fast it will be able to move in the face of shifting winds.

Power systems are complex. Red tape can be an explicit form of work control or surveillance. Other forms of power may be more subtly culture-based—rooted in norms, customs, and traditions. These can contribute to rigid and inflexible systems that require approval chains, community consensus, and/or access to time-consuming, exclusive, and/or expensive credentialing, all of which get in the way of creative problem-solving and responsiveness to a dynamic environment.

Creating truly resilient systems that can adapt and evolve as conditions change will require us to take a closer look at the ways in which we've baked old expectations into technologies, methods of skill development, and language that makes some decisions and behaviors easier and more accepted than others. Examining those practices and coming up with alternatives is easier in systems that are also open and where information is readily accessible to make nuanced and thoughtful choices.

When those conditions exist, it becomes much easier to set a shared direction and inspire people to get there together. Ironically, many leaders desire the benefits of agile, adaptive systems and promote the idea of prototyping and rapid innovation but try to accomplish those ideals via models of management that actively get in the way of the very creativity they covet.

As we saw in the last chapter, systems and structures that make it hard for information to flow freely can inhibit trust.

When leaders don't get the information or the context necessary to connect the dots between relevant insights, it interferes with their ability to pivot and adjust to changing circumstances. And we don't live in a world where circumstances are unchanging.

When we rely on strict rules over smart principles, we end up with real challenges like health care information that is excruciatingly hard to share between providers, resulting in gaps in care and agonizing experiences for patients and families. To understand, interpret, and use insurance policies, we require people to be able to read and understand complex legal documents.

We build a criminal justice system that doles out the stiffest penalties to those who can least afford legal representation, not to those whose crimes have the biggest impact on communities. We defend things because they are familiar or because we can't imagine an alternative, rather than remembering what we were out to solve for in the first place.

These challenges aren't just frustrating, they are expensive and time-consuming, and they dumb down creativity, imposing a system where people are made to enforce rules they know don't serve. When employees are not empowered to make changes or trusted to align their adjustments to strategy and trajectory, they are left telling patients, parents, customers, and citizens that they are just following policy, or just doing what the boss told them.

Today, strategic leadership is an act of rapid prototyping unto itself.[103] The pace at which things are prone to change can invite a range of responses—we can try to wrap our arms around a problem and simplify and dissect it (which usually means we miss the big picture); we can keep our eye on the horizon and hope that we can be responsive to whatever emerges; or we can find the productive tension created by living in the face of multiple potential outcomes and iterate our way forward.

We can test and learn our way into the future.

Since the early 1990s, Peter Senge and his colleagues have argued that companies that cultivate the five disciplines[104] of learning will thrive while others struggle to respond and adapt in a world where information is proliferating.

Systems become truly agile when we align around a shared vision and also cultivate the ability to connect the dots and look at things from multiple perspectives. If no one can see the whole, we've got to learn to both share and receive input and feedback that helps us adapt our way to better. In organizations made up of living, breathing humans, being nimble requires personal resilience and the ability to identify when change is needed. We must stay the course when that's what is called for and not be too buffeted by the winds of change.

It is so easy to fall into the go-go-go mode of squeezing in one more thing or chasing (or imposing) one last deadline, but a leader's ability to be adaptive is directly tied to their capacity for presence.

Being in the Now

Eckhart Tolle reminds us that every challenge is only ever solved from the present moment. We can't go back and change the past, and whatever futures we might imagine haven't happened yet. There is only now.[105] Most spiritual traditions include some form of reflective pause as a practice for connecting with or returning to one's higher self. When we can quiet the chatter in our minds, we increase our capacity for discernment.

As we saw earlier, when we are anxious or fearful, our bodies trigger responses that get our heart rates rising and our adrenaline coursing. To disrupt that reactive cycle, Pema Chodron,[106] Deepak Chopra,[107] and many others who have dedicated their lives to studying age-old practices of mindfulness, recommend conscious breathing, the simple practice of tuning into and noticing the inhales and exhales occurring in the present. Even newer institutions like modern militaries recognize the power of box breathing (putting one's attention on and counting out an even inhale-hold-exhale-hold pattern) to calm nerves and improve outcomes in the most stressful of circumstances. Navy Seals and fast-tech entrepreneurs alike know that intentional breathing gives them an edge.[108]

Using the word BREATH as a mantra reminds us that we have many resources at our disposal for finding our way back to the present moment (the only place from which we can be adaptive). Whenever we find ourselves a little off-center, we can tune into how we are *Being*, make time for *Reflection*, get some *Exercise*, reconnect with our *Aspirations*, confront how our *Time* is allocated, and tune into our *Heart*.

Being: When we focus on how we are *being* vs. what we are *doing*, we find we have a wider range of choices available to us. When we are in doing mode, we adjust project plans, revise timelines, and make sure we know where to direct our ire if things don't go according to plan. When we take that first inhale and look at how we want to show up, what impact we want to have, and how we might be connected, we find space to listen deeply, practice acceptance, and cultivate empathy.

Years ago, a leader I worked with taught me to recover my connection to who and how I was being by thinking of a transition ritual that would help me wake up to where I was in the moments when autopilot might otherwise take over. Any little habit or ritual that is already a part of your day is something you can bring your awareness to. There isn't a particular magic to what the activity is—it's the noticing that matters. Instead of repeating something mindlessly, we can bring mindfulness to it, and reconnect with how we are being (and ask ourselves whether that state is aligned with our intentions).

What daily habits can you shift from automatic to intentional?

Reflection: How often do you make space to meditate, journal, or talk to a friend or colleague? As leaders, pausing to reflect on successes and setbacks, and creating occasions to collect and review our thoughts, helps keep us alert, aware, and focused on where we want to go and what habits or patterns in our life are serving us well (or not). I've been a poorly disciplined and episodic journal-keeper throughout my life. I often journal while on retreat and have at various important turning points over time, but I've also spent far too many years secretly wishing I was consistently keeping a daily diary of some sort. Eventually, I realized that that mode of reflection just wasn't for me—it didn't fit seamlessly enough into my life to be sustainable.

And then I started noticing and appreciating all the habits of reflection I had built! I have books of poetry scattered everywhere, along with card decks that include prompts, quotes, or questions I find helpful for resetting my brain when it gets stuck in a swirl. At the very least, these things create a little disruptive pause and often help me look at something I have been stuck on with a fresh perspective.

I also have routines of reflection with friends and team members—regular habits of taking stock that help keep things in perspective.

What routines of reflection work best for you?

Exercise is so easy to ignore or let fall by the wayside, especially when we get wrapped up in an important project. A sedentary lifestyle leads to sluggish thinking. When we aren't moving our bodies, we don't have access to the best of our brains. Even brief moments of standing or short walks can help us shift out of reactivity and tap into our more creative minds. Whether you are an elite athlete or have physical conditions that make it hard to get out and about, exercise is not about your overall health or a training regimen—it's about learning to move your body in ways that bring you back to presence and engage the innovation centers in your brain.

Look around your environment for ways to bring intentional movement into your day-to-day routine, not just in formal workouts. Using a standing desk, taking a few flights of stairs between meetings instead of waiting for the elevator, or scheduling a walking meeting are all simple ways to re-energize throughout the day. Build a dance-party playlist and put it on shuffle whenever you need to get unstuck. If your mobility is restricted, keeping hand weights nearby or even raising and lowering your arms periodically can produce a similar benefit. Identifying these impromptu movement moments can help you build them in to any day, no matter how jam-packed the calendar, giving you the reset needed to lead better.

Where can you build intentional movement into your everyday routine?

Aspiration: Getting clear on the purposes or commitments you care about helps ground and remind you of what really matters. It's easy to get lost in the weeds of a project or hung up on an interaction that didn't go the way we wish it might have. Whether our leadership field of play is a boardroom, a ball field, a playroom, or a community meeting, it always helps to keep our eye on the prize and remember what we are steering toward.

If you've used the VIABLE mantra to establish your vision and ideals, these things, taken together, become a succinct way to frame what it is you aspire to: where you are going and what commitments are important to you along the way. Some people find it helpful to create a vision board or mind movie to keep their dreams in front of them. For others, a sticky note on the bathroom mirror or their loved one's picture on a desk does the trick.

How will you keep your aspiration front and center?

Time: How do you spend it? Does it energize and enliven or deplete you? Our whole lives are made up of moments and we don't get do-overs, so bringing intentionality to how we spend the minutes and hours in our days has a big influence on how we spend the years of our life. This means bringing attention both to what you spend time on and how that time makes you feel.

Try this for a week: Notice hourly how you are spending your time. Make note of the things that go well or give you joy and those that are draining; then make small adjustments that allow you to make time for things that are important but not urgent; and make space for things you love and people who nourish you. There isn't a "right" way to do this; find your own rhythm and a routine that serves you.

How can you create or give more space to things that enliven you? How can you limit things that drain you? What can you stop doing or what can you ask for help with?

Heart: Learning to connect with and lead from our heart may be the most potent strategy for becoming more connected leaders. How you make people feel is one of your most powerful leadership levers. As leaders, how we are feeling ourselves and how connected to what our heart is telling us is directly correlated to how we impact and influence others.

As the findings from fields like neurophysics, psychophysiology, and neurocardiology find their way into the mainstream, we are learning that the heart has its own intelligence, and that the heart and brain act on and influence one another in remarkable ways.

This research suggests that it's not just a triggering of our primal, reactive brain that stimulates an increase in heart rate and blood pressure; the heart is able to send messages TO the brain, not just receive them.[109]

If this idea intrigues you, it is a rapidly evolving area of leadership study that I encourage you to investigate more deeply. Learning how to tap into the wisdom of your heart and foster heart-brain coherence is a powerful skillset for leaders at all levels. How can you connect more deeply with the wisdom of your heart?

BREATH Mantra

When we are distracted or dislocated, our best selves are often out of reach. This mantra reminds us that there are many paths back to presence and gives us options, at any moment, for returning to the now.

Chapter Six—Being Adaptive

Am I *BEING* the change I wish to create?

What mode of *REFLECTION* suits me best?

How can I *EXERCISE* to energize?

What *ASPIRATION* keeps me inspired and motivated?

Am I spending my *TIME* on what matters most?

Is my *HEART* leading the way? Am I listening?

Chapter Six—Being Adaptive

The Power of Presence

Beyond the well-documented biological reasons for cultivating "presencing practices" that allow us to root ourselves in the now, there is substantial evidence that, in any given challenge we observe in a system, the dynamics of the whole exist.[110] When we focus too narrowly, we may address the symptoms of the issue but miss the network of interactions that routinely conspire to keep something in place. And our quick fixes then serve to reproduce or exacerbate the root cause rather than solving for it.

Getting groups of people to do great things together requires a broader view than this. When we are more present, we are better able to zoom out and see how the parts affect, and are affected by, the whole. As leaders we are better able to help team members see how their piece of the puzzle fits.

Some of the winningest coaches of all time know that this works.

Phil Jackson won a record eleven championships as the head coach of the Chicago Bulls and Los Angeles Lakers. He led different teams, with different strengths, full of different personalities, to victory over the span of nearly two decades.[111] Early on in Jackson's career, outlets like ESPN tagged him a Zen Master[112] because his approach differed from many of his contemporaries, who used winner-takes-all strategies of intimidation to motivate their teams.

Jackson, instead, drew from contemplative Zen traditions and Native American practices to cultivate clearheadedness amidst the chaos of a game.[113] This allowed superstars like Michael Jordan, Scottie Pippen, Shaquille O'Neil, and Kobe Bryant to channel their individual greatness into team success.

In *The Last Dance*,[114] a documentary about Michael Jordan and the rise of the Chicago Bulls' dominance in the 1990s, Mark Vancil, one of Jordan's biographers, highlighted the impact of this way of being:

> "Most people struggle to be present. . . . Most people live in fear because they project the past. Michael's a mystic. He was never anywhere else. His gift was not that he could jump high, run fast, shoot a basketball; his gift was that he was completely present and that was the separator . . . . A big downfall of a lot of players who are otherwise gifted is thinking about failure. Michael didn't allow what he couldn't control to get inside his head. He would say, 'Why would I think about missing a shot I haven't even taken yet?'"

The field of Conscious Leadership captures the essence of this philosophy by encouraging leaders to examine where they are "above the line," to be conscious, present, and aware of current events and circumstances without turning them into stories that have a propensity to take on a life of their own, and that inevitably pull us out of presence and into a whole host of imagined dramas.

One of the principles I've found most powerful in this body of work is the notion that each of us should take 100% responsibility[115] for our response to the circumstances we find ourselves in. This doesn't mean that we ignore broader dynamics or hold people or organizations blameless for the impact of their actions, but rather remind ourselves that we are always the one having any given reaction and that how we respond in the face of whatever it is, is up to us.

This is also a powerful presencing move. Change can only happen from where we are. Getting tangled up in anger, frustration, or despair about what has already occurred, or worrying about things that haven't happened yet, only serves to pull us out of the now and makes us less able to adapt effectively.

This impulse to pause and gather ourselves is something we are born with but somehow seem to forget along the road to finding our way in the world, so we need to find the people and spaces that help us remember.

The best teachers in our lives are not always experts or scholars or gurus but those who model something that we can apprentice. I have two children who are very different. My son was born "in motion," always on the move—rolling and scooting and reaching as early as he could manage it. Being anywhere near a busy street with him when he was a toddler was a stressful event, as he darted about this way and that. He was not yet three when he gave up napping on most days, preferring to be active instead.

I didn't realize it at the time, but I often was simply trying to keep pace with him. Over the years he had to work to learn to find his "calm in the storm."

My daughter, on the other hand, arrived with an otherworldly capacity for stillness. She slept well, often putting herself down for a rest whenever she felt she needed one. I remember watching her in complete amazement in her early days.

I was already a student of yoga and conceptually understood the value of meditation and mindfulness, but she was presence incarnate.

This is a poem I wrote when she was just a few months old.

Poetic Pause
Zen Baby

Summer 2008

From the beginning, you were unhurried.

As I labored and strained you were calm; your heart rate hardly changing.

I grew anxious. You remained serene.

When you entered this world all wet and waxy, I smiled and cried.

You sighed and slept.

From the beginning you have been my counter point.

As I watch you sleep more soundly than I remember how, I marvel at you.

Your easy smile reminds me that life can be light.

My heart swells at your focused cry calling, "I know what I want."

"Children are our greatest teachers," I have often said.

What lessons do you have in store, I wonder?

You remind me to return to the breath when I am crazy.

You show me the restorative power of rest.

the KOAN method

You call me back to the present.

Every day, you embody the cycle of life.

Every day I delight in watching your life unfold and mourn the loss of yesterday.

You are mindfulness in motion.

In you I learn to hold lightly.

With you I discover I can notice and let go.

Your eyes close, lashes gently flutter.

Your breath slows and finds its rhythm.

From the beginning, you have been my Zen baby.

Until the end I'll watch and learn from you.

A KOAN Case Study: The Million Dollar Conversation

When we are in the "right now," we're able to adapt more readily because we are less tied to how things have always been, or to some idealized notion of how we want them to be. Remaining anchored to the past is one of the greatest inhibitors to organizational agility.

Several years ago, I did some consulting for a large insurance company that had just gone through an organization-wide process to define a new vision for its future. After many years of profitably providing traditional health coverage, they set out on a mission to focus more of their services on lifelong well-being—betting that focusing on improving the health and well-being of their members would be better for business in the long run. This was a clear shift in the company's mission, and senior leaders put a lot of time and energy into communicating the bold new intentions to the organization at-large via meetings, promotional materials, and live events.

At the same time, as a publicly traded company, the organization had financial targets to meet. Recognizing that their shift in strategic priorities would create some temporary revenue gaps, they set about a cost-cutting initiative that would allow the company to transition to the new mission-driven work without going into the red. For this initiative, each department leader was asked to come up with a reduced budget. While most responded with traditional methods like headcount reductions and salary freezes, a senior finance leader (we'll call her Linda) got creative.

Her approach was very KOAN and also ahead of its time.

Taking the company's new commitments to heart, Linda pulled her team together and invited them to consider how they could coordinate better or differently to cut costs in ways that were mission-aligned.

Could they save money while improving customer wellbeing? Could they cut $1M from their budget without resorting to staffing cuts they knew would undermine the mission?

The first move was to get the finance leads of individual units in conversation with one another. After several weeks of transparent information sharing and ideating, the team identified ways to reduce the length of a person's wait time in the call center, shorten the time it took to resolve claims, and standardize some of the technical systems used across departments.

The team projected these changes would increase efficiency and save more than $1.5 M without laying anyone off.

Proud of her team and their ability to devise an agile solution, Linda enthusiastically presented the approach to the executive team who were, initially, excited to see her bringing an even greater savings to the table than had been asked for.

In the weeks that followed, however, traditional methods of budgeting and reporting got in the way. Linda's innovative solution was treated as a onetime opportunity rather than as a recurring savings effort, which removed much of its actual saving power (not to mention its connection with the long-term mission). When Linda and her team argued that their collaborative method of organizing and brainstorming could be used in other departments to save even more money, they were dismissed in favor of more familiar strategies, namely salary freezes and layoffs.

In developing her solution, Linda took all of the KOAN principles to heart: she was *Kind* in genuinely caring about her team and demonstrating that they mattered both to her and to the organization; she was *Open* in her transparent sharing of the challenge of needing to reduce costs, and in the way she encouraged cross-functional information sharing; she was *Adaptive* in the way she involved her team in creative problem-solving, and in finding a solution that would serve the evolving challenges of an organization in transition; and she brought forward a solution that had *Network* implications for how to better connect the dots across lines of business.

Sadly, these well-informed and well-intended efforts collided with older ways of organizing that undermined these mission-driven benefits. Well-worn notions of how to achieve cost savings interfered with an ability to seize the opportunity to test a new way that might have modeled new possibilities for the future.

Ultimately, Linda was asked to use a more traditional form of saving money and make staffing cuts. Not only was this at odds with the well-being mission and demoralizing to the team that had been proud and excited to deliver a strategy that avoided the need for such cuts, the layoffs she was ordered to make delivered fewer dollars in savings to the bottom line.

The situation went from a mission-driven win-win to a mission-damaging lose-lose. The mission wasn't the problem, the systems meant to carry it out were. Examples like this are far too common as our ideals for leading in more purpose-driven ways collide with the calcified systems and outdated structures of our organizations.

Of course, systems don't exist on their own, they only persist because people create and recreate them over and over again in practice. In this case, even as the organization was setting its intention to change, some of the most senior leaders turned to familiar but harsher and less effective strategies, instead of embracing new solutions that were more innovative and mission-aligned.

If we want to make the most of mission-driven leadership and achieve the full measure of breakthrough impact we believe it can have, we need to move beyond developing individual leaders and look seriously at how we are organizing and rewarding people to get good work done together.

Linda and her team's efforts highlight both the potential inherent in breakthrough leadership and the pitfalls of applying its methods inside organizations that haven't yet updated their systems to align with mission-related strategy. While Linda and her team were a touch ahead of their time—early adopters on their organization's journey of transformation—over the next several years, that organization took their new commitments to heart to deliver breakthrough results.

Leaders and teams worked to make many meaningful changes to how work got done to foster exactly the kind of innovation and leadership that Linda had modeled from the beginning. Her methods of collaborating across departments to find those early savings became more widespread. Even more importantly, the mindset of using the mission as a filter for critical financial investments and decision-making became more and more common.

Agile Evolution

Despite decades of business literature calling for more organizational agility, there are still many spheres where change comes slowly, and often still carry industrial-age assumptions and practices even when they arrive. For large publicly traded companies in particular, there are still heavy traditional constraints to navigate, including quarterly earnings calls that favor short-term gains over long-term mission-driven investments that might foster sustainability for the long haul. And public sector organizations are often beset by bureaucracy while nonprofits are beholden to traditional funding and board structures. More progress is needed.

When the COVID-19 pandemic forced a global shutdown in early 2020, businesses of all shapes and sizes, across industries and geographies, found their business models disrupted overnight. Many didn't survive or have been fundamentally and permanently changed.

One organization that fared well in the face of disruption, however, was consumer product giant Unilever. In 2012, the company launched an open innovation platform to crowdsource solutions to a wide range of challenges, from climate action and protecting and regenerating natural resources to improved standards of living and reimagining the future of work.[116]

The value of this model is that Unilever extends their reach out into a global entrepreneurial marketplace in ways that allow them to discover breakthrough ideas faster than more traditional corporate research and development typically allow. Meanwhile, they also nurture and cultivate partnerships by providing early-stage funding in emerging technologies, leveraging the company's laboratory infrastructure, iterating and refining products in ways that small organizations might not be able to, and identifying potential supply chain partners and acquisition opportunities.

The platform through which potential partners can discover challenges and submit ideas invites people in by saying:

> *If we think we can do it alone, we are not thinking big enough.*
>
> *We're innovating with partners to bring together bright minds, big ideas and disruptive technology. Are you working on something that could match our collective ambitions? Let's connect.*

This cultural commitment to innovation and existing investments in a global network of partners allowed the company to pivot its focus toward high-need, high-demand products during the pandemic and remain profitable during a year that saw many competitors fare much worse. In their 2020 annual report, Unilever attributed some of this success to the emphasis it had put on building "a purpose-led, future-fit organization and growth culture."[117]

This mindset permeated the organizational culture and enabled 70,000 global employees to shift to working remotely almost overnight, while maintaining data security. Having foreseen the potential of remote collaboration before the pandemic, the company had made significant investments in connective technologies that enabled its office-based workers to seamlessly transition to a virtual work environment.[118]

Chapter Six—Being Adaptive

This ability to rapidly pivot HOW work got done allowed Unilever's teams to focus their energies on making critical business adjustments that were important to both company health and public safety. Where hand sanitizer was once a relatively small portion of Unilever's portfolio, with two factories producing a collective 700,000 units per month, by May of 2020, two months into the global shutdown, 61 factories around the world were producing more than 100 million units monthly.[119]

When a big change occurs, whether as a happy surprise or a looming crisis, those who can best respond are likely to be those who have already invested in strong and trusting relationships and built systems that bend and flex well. Rigid systems are not resilient, but those who have built agility into their DNA find that disruptions in the external environment become catalysts for organizational evolution while others struggle to stay afloat or fail altogether.

Earlier, we learned the power of setting a VIABLE Strategy™ to align teams around a shared vision, core ideals, and actionable approach. We also saw that part of the power in defining an approach over a more detailed plan is that it allows the team to focus on where it is headed, and on the key milestones that might indicate progress along the way, instead of on more stepwise timelines that hold up poorly to changing conditions.

The second half of the VIABLE mantra is where the power to adapt is really unleashed, where you can set yourself up for resilience and build cycles of learning and transforming into your work.

Stay Relevant by Evolving

As a reminder the VIABLE model becomes a helpful scorecard of sorts:

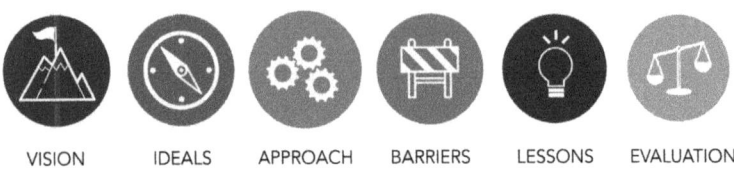

Figure 7: Integrated Work's VIABLE Strategy Model

We have explored how to approach answering these questions openly and transparently in ways that engaged stakeholders broadly, but resilient organizations that adapt well to change are also good at course correction—the art of staying on track when conditions change.

By identifying potential barriers early, and troubleshooting them proactively, any system can learn to learn. This builds confidence not only in the ability to respond to any given scenario, but to the notion that whatever comes along, there are ways to approach it that will yield breakthroughs in service of a shared vision.

Below, we'll tackle these adaptive engines:

Identifying BARRIERS and how to overcome them. Most groups have an easy time coming up with worst-case scenarios—all the things that might get in the way of a vision being realized. These generally include some versions of lack of funding, lack of support, unfavorable conditions, and so on. Many traditional SWOT (Strengths, Weaknesses, Opportunities, and Threats) analyses are designed to surface these challenges, but too often the good stuff gets treated as though it is completely distinct from the bad stuff. This can leave people feeling like their strengths will carry them through UNLESS threats arise or leave them worrying that they won't be able to take advantage of opportunities BECAUSE their weaknesses might undermine them. This exercise pulls people out of the present and generates a context of worry that is often at odds with creative problem-solving.

I've found it much more impactful to give teams a time-bound window in which to brainstorm all the BARRIERS they can imagine that would interfere with their goals. For the first exercises, it's best not to overanalyze and no detailed research is required. This is about surfacing what people are worried about.

Once that brainstorming is done, it's helpful to do some gut-checking and identify which scenarios are most likely and which might be most disruptive. Then, back in the present, I invite the group to problem-solve what they would do if a given issue happened right then. What if a funder or key customer called and cancelled a major commitment? What if a key supplier went out of business or couldn't meet your demand? What if attendance at a key fundraising event was half of what you were hoping for?

Sometimes people panic a little for a moment or two, but then they quickly discover that they already know what they would do! They'd call in partners or allies, tap reserves, shift priorities, and together they would come up with a solution. Often this exercise does reveal real potential pain points—a brittle supply chain or overreliance on too few funding sources, for example.

Now, the team is not in panic and paralysis mode, but in innovative problem-solving mode. Rather than worrying about what might happen way off in the future, they can focus on what they can do in the present to increase resilience and agility. Engaging in this kind of barrier-busting activity creates an embodied experience of rising to a challenge together, as a team. This builds important muscle memory for real crisis moments and fosters curiosity and a drive to iterate, learn, and improve.

Naming LESSONS that will help you turn setbacks into successes. The most adaptive and resilient organizations are great at learning and building routines of feedback and growth into their systems. While "fail fast" became a tech industry slogan for many years, the goal is not really to run around making a mess of things. Instead, organizations can learn to "fail smart"[120] by learning fast.

Once barriers have been identified, it's helpful to think about what will be helpful (or necessary) to learn on the way to achieving the vision. What new insight, knowledge, or expertise will be necessary? How can we shift into inquiry to accelerate learning?

This kind of intentional, rapid learning is made harder by hierarchy but flourishes in environments with nimble cross-functional teams that have been empowered to experiment and iterate their way to success. This is made easier in environments where members feel trusted and have access to the data that affects their work. In retail environments, for example, stores that empower local outlets to choose how to stock the shelves and are given the sales data to know what is working and not, can make much more nimble adjustments than a team of analysts reviewing spreadsheets from a distant corporate office. When rewards are also aligned to those metrics, the system is set up to evolve itself.

Using methods of EVALUATION that allow you to gather feedback and adapt. While most planning models include some emphasis on metrics, I have found it particularly powerful to explore questions of evaluation in the context of organizational learning. Too often metrics are set for convenience (because the data is easy to gather) or because some things have historically been measured (who was the top sales performer last quarter?).

In a world where what gets measured gets managed, however, it serves us well to be more intentional about what purposes are served by our evaluation—how will looking at data in this way or sharing them with these people help us learn what we need to know to get to where we want to go?

By first asking what we need to learn, the kinds of things we become interested in assessing often change. Participation and attendance data is less interesting if what we care about is impact. Ranking data is less meaningful if we are trying to motivate collaboration and foster innovative team-based solutions.

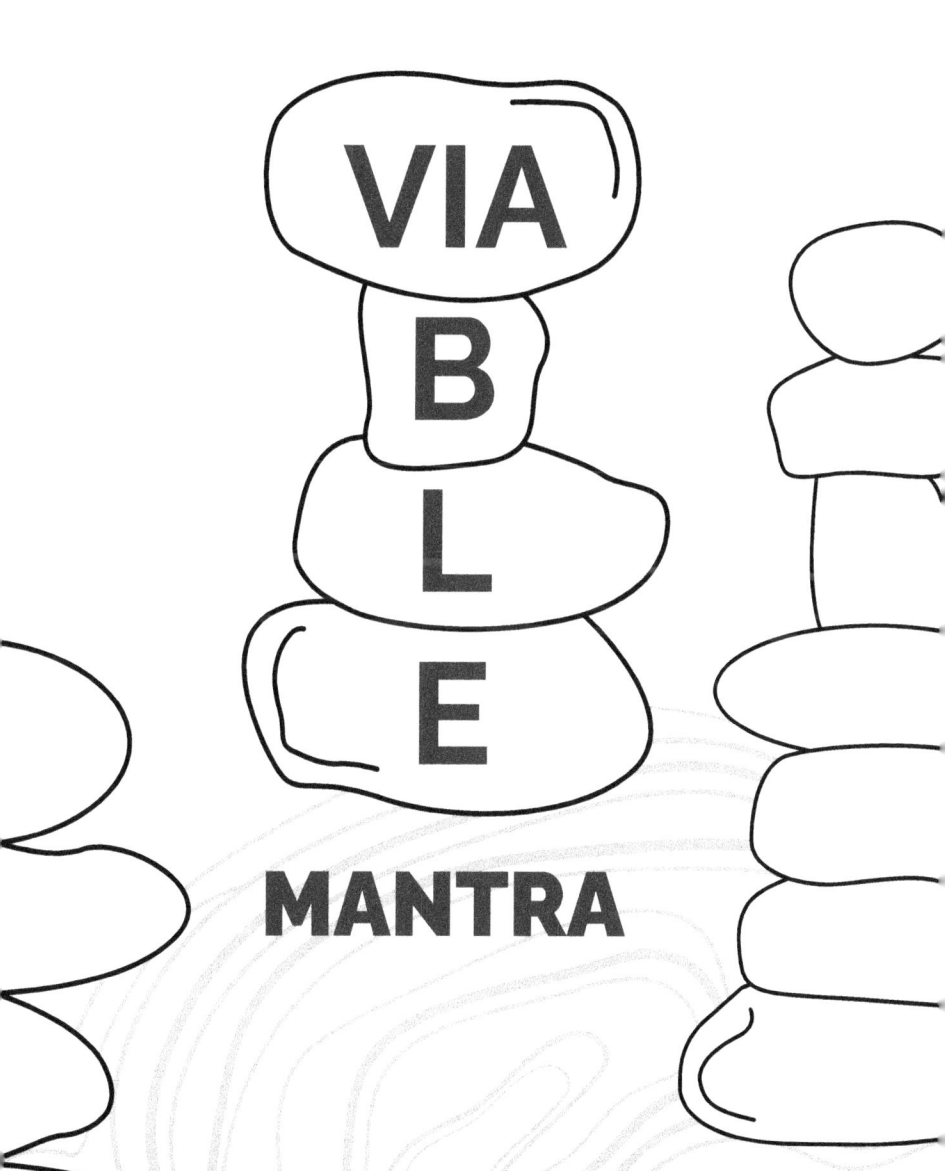

(VIA)BLE Mantra

True agility comes from faith that we can adjust our course in the face of challenges. This mantra helps us proactively predict what might interfere with progress and cultivate a learning mindset that strengthens creativity to keep us moving in the direction of our goals, even as the world shifts around us.

Chapter Six—Being Adaptive

What **BARRIERS** might get in your way; how might you overcome them?

Have you identified **LESSONS** that will help you turn setbacks into successes?

What methods of **EVALUATION** will allow you to gather feedback and adapt?

Can you get as good at generating solutions as at predicting setbacks?

What capacity do you need to build, or insights do you need to succeed?

Are you measuring the things that matter most to your desired outcomes?

Chapter Six—Being Adaptive

Changing the metrics that we use to tell a story about who we are and how we are doing takes intentionality and effort but is often one of the greatest levers available for creating the "aha!" moment that shifts a group from stuck to breakthrough.

Done well, this can also rewrite our understanding of how to *Nurture Networks of Relationship* in ways that help us reach our goals.

Chapter Seven

Nurture Networks of Relationship

Fight for the things that you care about. But do it in a way that will lead others to join you.

~ Ruth Bader Ginsburg

Many of today's organizations and institutions still run on models of leadership that were designed to contend with physical distance and slow communication. Hierarchies were efficient ways of cascading information when it had to be moved by small numbers of people across large distances. The volume of information was low, and the time it took to move an idea from one person or place to another was significant. In today's world, everyone can have access to the same information if given the same access to resources (which are, of course, not actually evenly distributed). Today, hierarchies mostly serve to maintain that old imbalance, baking inequity into systems that reinforce and exacerbate separation.

In the industrial age, we learned to create efficiency by breaking things down into their component parts and then putting them together on an assembly line. If you know the exact specification for every part that makes up the product, this can work well and save time, as each person learns their part of the job and doesn't worry about another's. But even in this model, things fall apart the more complex the end result is and the more we need it to flex and change in the face of evolving conditions.

In our highly customized, rapidly adapting world, models made for machines are often too rigid; eventually living, breathing people get squeezed by systems not built for them. Moreover, rigid hierarchies are notoriously bad at handling transformation. As organizational and leadership scholar John Kotter has remarked:

> *The challenge is that, at both a philosophical and a practical level, the Hierarchy (with its management processes) opposes change. It strives to eliminate anomalies, standardize processes, solve short-term problems, and achieve stopwatch efficiency within its current mode of operating.*
>
> *In a sense, the crowning accomplishment of the Hierarchy and its management processes is the enterprise on autopilot, everyone ideally situated as a cog whirring on a steady, unthinking, and predictable machine.*[121]

Chapter Seven—Nurture Networks of Relationship

Over the last 30 or so years, leaders have begun to recognize that connecting people to the mission of their organization or community, and demonstrating care for employees or members, could be a competitive advantage. Groups and organizations that positioned themselves as purpose-driven began to attract better talent and set themselves apart.

This only works over the long term, though, if the systems are built to be resilient and actively solicit input, act on insights, and leverage networks of relationship both in and outside of the organization to make things better.

Over the last several years, we've seen up close where brittle systems fail, how communities of care rally to ride out even the worst of times, and what happens when espoused values don't match lived realities.

Ultimately, when system-scale problems are solved idiosyncratically and in isolation, the outcomes are less creative, produce poorer results, and tend to be less equitable as the impacts can vary widely.

While business schools and professional development programs have touted the benefits of more purpose- or mission-driven leadership for many years, we haven't done nearly as good a job at evolving our systems to maximize that potential. When we revert to organizing systems that are isolated rather than connected and try to solve challenges that exist at the scale of societies inside of silos, we tend to get suboptimal results.

It is hard to change hearts and minds when the systems and structures are still stuck in old ways of working. For the most part, people don't resist change itself—in fact, we humans often go looking for change when we commit to a life partner, have children, make significant purchases, or move across the country or around the world.

What most of us are actually afraid of is being unsuccessful or irrelevant in an uncertain future. We fear loss of status, competence, and comfort.

When we see ourselves as interdependent and interconnected, we can both tap the collective wisdom to come up with better, more resilient, common-good solutions from the outset AND make change easier as people feel supported, connected, and less alone as they step into the future.

If groups or organizations espouse caring values but don't adjust and adapt their systems and processes to support these changing ways of leading and working, they create a disconnect that can erode faith in, and commitment to, that system.

When systems are built on a me-first, everyone-for-themselves model, we get results that favor the few over the many. And, because historical power dynamics are deeply woven into many of our existing systems, we end up perpetuating inequity and deepening division instead of nurturing networks of connection.

One of the most striking and visible examples of this is the development of the interstate highway system. While networks of roads may appear to connect communities, a closer look reveals how their construction in the 1950s and 1960s served to displace large numbers of communities of color in favor of predominantly white businesses and landowners. A particularly striking example of this was the complete dissolution of Overtown, a vibrant Miami neighborhood of more than 10,000 people, mostly African American, who were dispersed and dislocated to build a section of I-95. This came after decades of efforts by local white business owners to move Black residents out so that their own business district could expand.[122]

Fundamental infrastructure decisions like these have long-term consequences for communities as water and power lines tend to follow transportation networks and can lock in more favorable services and access for some communities while leaving others to contend with inferior resources for generations.[123] Because big companies tend to settle where infrastructure is strong (and are often offered major tax incentives for doing so), these infrastructure disparities have a compounding effect, as the best jobs go to the already best-resourced communities, which grows their tax base and funds investments in everything from schools to recreation facilities.

Stanford researcher Nicholas Bloom, found that one of the greatest drivers of overall wealth inequality is the pay gap not just between CEOs and workers in some of the world's largest firms, but between firms themselves. Those who work for "top" companies (located in well-resourced neighborhoods and cities) often make several times more in salary, benefits, and bonuses than those doing similar work elsewhere.

Disrupting these disparities and restoring networks of relationship, connection, and mutual thriving takes intentionality. Some communities are getting creative about how to reimagine economic investments that reduce rather than exacerbate historical inequities. In 2022, New York Governor

Kathy Hochul signed the "Green CHIPS" program into law, sealing a deal between Empire State Development and Micron, an advance microchip manufacturer, to invest heavily in communities in and around Syracuse, New York, where it committed to building new factories. Rather than potentially dislocating communities and hiring lots of workers not already based in the region, the economic development deal included investments in the Central New York region,[124] including commitments to community-transforming activities like:

- Diverse Business Contracting and Utilization
- Providing Employment Opportunities for Diverse and Disadvantaged Populations
- Education and Workforce Pipeline Development
- Workforce Support Programs
- Community Engagement

Micron's decision to build its new facilities in this region came after more than a year of fierce competition from other cities. Ultimately, the ingenuity of the deal, including the opportunity to invest in cultivating a diverse workforce that had historically been largely underrepresented in semiconductor manufacturing, was attractive to the company,[125] resulting in a solution that had benefits for the organization, the community, and the broader economic environment in a part of the state hit hard when large scale manufacturing moved out in the early 20th century.

Imagine the impact to whole neighborhoods of raising the median household income by 50 or even 100 thousand dollars over the span of a few years.

The dozens of leaders, ranging from community organizers to state and local agency staff to senators and congressional representatives, who were involved in brokering the deal kept these commitments to community revitalization top of mind throughout the negotiations. It is leaders like these, who can stay present to purpose and steer true to their core commitments in a way that invites curiosity in the face of differences, that build the resilience to thrive over time.

The networks of people they attract and inspire are those that will prosper, not by dominating differences but by listening to them for the truly breakthrough solutions of tomorrow. This care-full curiosity sets both people and organizations up for lasting success.

The Way Forward

This is the true promise of embracing diversity in organizations—the radical innovation born from a group of people able to see all sides, together. Doing this well takes intentionality at many levels. I like using JEDI (Justice, Equity, Diversity, Inclusion) as a mantra to remember to keep the pursuit of justice out front. Simply put, the inclusion of different perspectives helps us discover solutions that are better for more people.

Justice is a pursuit that includes fostering a world that acknowledges its *history* and is working to build a flourishing future. A Just world has equitable and sustainable distribution of resources; and all members are physically and psychologically safe, secure, recognized, and treated with respect.

So, when we put justice out front, we examine how policies, procedures, practices, mores, and norms influence the distribution of resources and whether that distribution is balanced and fair. We focus our efforts on *correcting or disrupting* things that cause unfair, unethical, or unwarranted treatment of a person or group.

> "Justice is what love looks like in public."[126]
> ~Cornell West

Equity is the process that levels the playing field, bringing balance of opportunity such that negative impact is not tied to identity. Equity is the scale that examines how things operate and impact groups.

The quest for equity seeks assurance that policies, processes, and resources are applied *fairly* toward everyone within a setting in a way that acknowledges and adjusts for *unique* backgrounds and circumstances. Equity recognizes the power of being adaptive in the face of difference.

> "True equity starts with ensuring that everyone has access to the most basic of needs."[127]
> ~Mikki Kendall

Diversity is about ensuring the *representation* of all stakeholders *impacted* by the matter at hand—both its process and outcome. It is not just about race, but the full spectrum of core identities that have social capital: age, ability, gender, race, religion, sex, sexuality, national or political identity, and other social identities represented in communities, institutions, cultures, and society.

Diversity speaks to those aspects that are largely unchangeable, those not contingent on behavior but on a sense of self. Diversity is what gives us access to fresh perspectives and grows our ability to see an issue from multiple angles.

> "You cannot undo a problem with the consciousness that created it."[128]
> ~Heather McGhee

Inclusion is what makes diversity powerful. It is the principles, practices, policies, procedures, and actions that foster voice—where we can actually begin to hear each other across our differences. Inclusion abides by the platinum rule "Do unto others as they would do for themselves."

Inclusion is the practice of providing access to opportunities and resources for groups of people that might otherwise be marginalized based on identities. It expands opportunities and resources so that more people can *contribute* effectively and feel valued and worthy of *belonging*.

> "Inclusion is the only safety if we are to have a peaceful world."[129]
> ~Pearl S. Buck

JEDI Mantra

No "great" solutions work for only some of the people, some of the time. This mantra keeps us present to places where inequity might interfere with optimal outcomes and helps us explore what real breakthroughs require.

Chapter Seven—Nurture Networks of Relationship

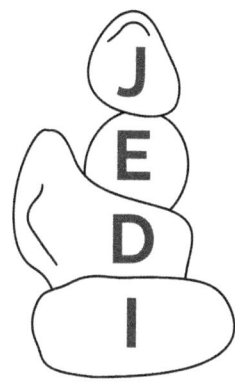

JUSTICE—Does the "how and what" of decisions and actions foster flourishing?

Will more people be better off as a result of these decisions?

EQUITY—Does the action we are taking ensure opportunity is evenly distributed?

Are we working proactively to redress past harms or disparities?

DIVERSITY—Are we attending to the full range of identities and histories held by people within a setting?

Whose perspectives and experiences might yield fresh insight or get us unstuck?

INCLUSION—Are we conscious of how a diverse range of people are represented in processes prior to actions and outcomes?

Is everyone valued for their contributions? Do they feel safe to bring ideas forward?

Connecting Across Differences

When we come together across differences with curiosity and interest, we sometimes discover echoes of ourselves in the least expected places.

The answers to our challenges will rarely come from external factors, but rather by looking within ourselves, digging into the heart of the conflict itself, and discovering the inherent potential of groups of people to come up with their own best solutions. These answers tend to arise in community when we see ourselves as interconnected instead of as individual and isolated.

One of the things that struck me in my early travels was how similar human circumstances and challenges are, no matter the place, and how unique the solutions sometimes are. As a child and teenager, one of the things that always struck me was the different ways of supporting (or not supporting) unhoused people from place to place.

In one city you might see someone huddled in a doorway, shunned and outcast by society, their bare feet oozing from open sores. Elsewhere, creative solutions to feeding and housing these community members are a symbol of cultural pride. In one place, the individual was seen as the problem, while in another place, the lack of food and housing was the issue and needed to be addressed.

When we see ourselves as belonging to a network of interdependence, we find more creative solutions to all manner of challenges. In many U.S. cities, homeless encampments are hotly debated at city council meetings. Most solutions still focus on central soup kitchens and temporary shelters that may provide some support for a night or a week but do nothing to address the underlying social dynamics that perpetuate the problem.

Some cities and organizations, however, are taking a much more human-centered approach and are finding great success by using community-based problem-solving principles rooted in a recognition of our shared humanity and in-it-togetherness.[130] Around the world, more than 150 million people are unhoused, and many others live in tenuous conditions. More and more communities are beginning to see homelessness as a housing problem, not a people problem, and they are taking a housing-first approach to helping people get back on their feet.[131]

Vienna, Austria, provides free and subsidized housing right downtown (not on the outskirts of town where a "nuisance" can be hidden) because the easy access to public transportation in center-city supports residents finding employment and getting to and from work. In Helsinki, Finland, no one sleeps on the streets. Unlike many communities with strict standards people must meet to become eligible for housing programs—often related to substance abuse or employment—the Finnish capital provides unconditional permanent access to housing. The city understands that creating conditions of safety and connection, and providing access to shelter, food, and running water, are key success factors in overcoming addiction and finding permanent employment. So, it provides housing first and then offers the support needed to overcome other challenges.

In the U.S., the Department of Veterans Affairs has recognized the value of this approach:

Housing First is an evidence-based, cost-effective approach to ending homelessness for the most vulnerable and chronically homeless individuals. The Housing First model prioritizes housing and then assists the veteran with access to health care and other supports that promote stable housing and improved quality of life. The model does not try to determine who is "housing ready" or demand treatment prior to housing. Instead, treatment and other support services are wrapped around veterans as they obtain and maintain permanent housing.[132]

Yet many communities persist in making people the problem and come up with siloed solutions when communities and networks might do better.

It is often the serendipitous collision of ideas that appear to be wildly at odds with one another that provokes some new insight or perspective that unlocks innovation.

When viewpoints are shared across cultures and from different experiences, we can find both common threads and breakthrough ideas.

Poetic Pause
The Tao of Dickinson
October 4, 2020

What might have passed
If Emily and Lao
Had sat down one day to Tea?

Her with her fine china and he with his little ceramic cup
She, drinking Earl Grey with just enough milk,
And he, savoring the clean aroma of his favorite Green.

What existential interludes might they have entertained?
Of death, and life, and our souls' great adventures . . .
Of what endures and what is fleeting, ephemeral.

"If I should die, and you should live," she might have begun.
"Each separate being in the universe returns to common
    source,"
Would have come the calm reply.

"A scone?" she might have offered.
"None for me, thanks,"
He would have said.

"The soul unto itself is an imperial friend,"
Emily might have declared,
As Lao nodded slowly, whispering—"to know oneself is
    true power."

She would have cocked her head, just so,
Stirring her cooling tea,
And looking into those wise old eyes.

the KOAN method

Quizzical now, she might have mused,
"It was not death, for I stood up,"
"Take away death, and there will no longer be life," he would
  have countered.

He would have held her gaze,
As she took the idea in,
And felt her growing calm.

"Hope is the thing with feathers, that perches in the soul,"
  Emily would have reflected, bringing her fingers lightly to
  the hollow of her throat.
"When I let go of what I am, I become what I might be," at
  last would have said he.

And thus, two butterflies might have gone out at noon,
Unhurried, yet accomplishing everything,
And then, together, been borne away.

A KOAN Case Study: It's Not Too Late (Networks to the Rescue)

Creating networks of relationship is where real magic begins to happen. As artificial silos begin to fall, we remember that we're not in "it" alone, and we begin to discover all manner of new, creative ideas and solutions. On the one hand, cultivating networks is well served by having tended to the other KOAN elements. Relationships flourish inside containers of care where transparency and trust are the norm, and where we cultivate presence instead of getting caught up in stories. One might argue that this is really an outgrowth of all the others. On the other hand, if we wait until we've gotten all of those other bits "just right" to relate to networks as the source of innovation and co-creation, we're still operating from a top-down, do-it-yourself mindset.

A network mindset is really the cornerstone of *the KOAN method*. If we want to get to the finish line first or find ourselves at the top of a hierarchical heap (until we get toppled), there are other approaches that will get us there faster. For problems that require collective problem-solving or that will benefit from a broader set of viewpoints, though, remembering our connectedness makes it easier to be kind, open, and adaptive. When we begin with empathy, give and receive openly, and cultivate resilience and agility, we realize that we don't do anything in isolation. We think of ourselves less as an entity (company, organization, team, community) and more as embedded in networks of mutuality.

Seth Godin has been an author and blogger for decades, with hundreds of thousands of social media followers and subscribers to his daily newsletter, "Seth's Blog." In October of

2021, Seth put out a call for readers who might be interested in working on a project idea he had, to pull "together a worldwide team of people who are interested in volunteering to contribute to the new Carbon Almanac."[133] He told his mailing list (a network whose trust and respect he'd cultivated over decades) that this would be a "zero-profit venture, a group effort designed to create a print and digital document that fills the vital niche between the cutting edge and apathy." At the time, 40 people from 20 countries that he'd hand-picked to seed the community were already at work on early pieces of the project. Anyone interested in the effort could fill out a form and Seth would connect with them.

I raised my hand, because that's what I do, and because this seemed like a way to contribute to a cause I already cared about, to connect with people from all over the world who cared about it too, and to work together in a way that seemed sure to push the envelope on co-creative collaboration. I filled out the form, saying I was in, and, if selected, that I'd bring members of my team along, too—believing we would all have something to contribute and a whole lot to learn.

A month later, I was excited to see the subject line: "Joining the Carbon Almanac Project" in my inbox. The invitation to join read, in part:

> More than 500 submissions from 25 countries. An author from the Middle East, a scientist from Nigeria, a TV journalist from New York... the one thing you all have in common is a desire to make an impact on a challenge faced by all of us.
>
> It wasn't easy to narrow down the list by more than 90%, but there you go.

I'd love to have you join us. We've been busy building the Almanac in smaller groups, so that we won't overwhelm everyone with too many folks joining in at once, but we're ready for you now and we need your help. . . .

Over the next several months, more than 300 of us from 41 countries researched, curated, compiled, drafted, edited, fact-checked, illustrated, and assembled *The Carbon Almanac*,[134] which became a bestseller in its genre even before it launched and earned the 2022 award for Most Insightful Data Book.[135] Once the book was assembled, we opened up the network again and have since drawn in thousands of people from more than a hundred countries, organizing ourselves around a core belief that "it's not too late" to address climate change if we lean into facts, connection, and action.

All of this was accomplished without any single official leader. Each of us stepped forward in different ways, as we were able, with the talents we could bring to bear on a joint challenge. A FastCompany article summarized the leadership like this, "Decisions and choices are made, but communication hinges on encouragement, trust, and mutual respect. It allows the group to be nimble—if something doesn't work, the group can adapt quickly and move to the next thing."[136] Networks are fundamentally better at solving system-scale problems than individuals or organizations that see themselves as more discrete or isolated.

In 1980, Ashoka was founded on the belief that anyone could make a meaningful difference to address social inequality if they were working in a context of community and support. They now invest annually in cultivating "a community of Fellows, Young Changemakers, Changemaker Institutions, and beyond who see that the world now requires everyone to *be a change-maker*—a person that sees themselves as capable of creating large-scale change."[137]

They call their theory of change "Collaborative Entrepreneurship Jiujitsu," and they use it to give social entrepreneurs all over the world the skills and connections that prepare them to tip the system toward justice and equality.

It is the power of these networks and the ability to leverage differences in service of the common good that makes them effective.

Nurturing Networks: Building for the Future, Now

Networks take nurturing to become strong, and one has to invest in cultivating them before they are needed. This is made easier if we already relate to ourselves as interdependent and interconnected. Some cultures have this spirit much more deeply woven into the fabric of their being than others, as we saw in the ways homelessness is addressed. Especially in countries or communities that value individualism more highly, it's helpful to cultivate practices that allow us to develop an embodied sense of ourselves as a part of, rather than apart from, others with whom we share common cause. Nurturing networks is not about seeing ourselves as an independent node trying to rally others to our cause, but about being able to appreciate the ways in which we affect and are at the effect of those around us.

I spent much of my early career in the highly individualized halls of academia and the still heavily male-dominated bastions of global commerce—often feeling like I was a lone voice in the wilderness, trying to be heard above the noise of taken-for-granted assumptions about "how things are." Those were often lonely years of sensing something was "off" in environments that fostered and favored solitary success even while championing collaboration or the value of high-performing teams.

Eventually, I went looking for a different kind of connection and found sisterhood in circles of women and with like-minded organizations and leaders. I learned to surround myself with people who also believed a different way was possible and soaked up everything I could learn from them and have tried to be generous with them in return.

This taught me the value of reciprocity and that, while networks flourish on generosity, they also require receptivity. If we are willing to give but not open to being influenced in return, there is a way in which we are still placing primacy on what we know or have. When we allow ourselves to be moved by others, we signal the value of what is on offer. For leaders, this principle comes to bear on how we think about growing and nurturing our teams and setting our organizations up for long lasting success.

If we are working toward building a more just and flourishing future, we can set up to **SUCCEED** by attending to the *Strategies for Understanding, Cultivating, and Championing Excellence in Equity and Diversity.*

Here's what this looks like in practice.

If the **strategies** we use presume that we know best, or that the future ought to look as much as possible like the past that we helped to build, we miss an opportunity to begin building the future now—to empower our teams to begin building something that we won't be a part of in the same way while we are still around to support, celebrate, and guide.

When we begin from curiosity and cultivate **understanding**, however, we create space for creativity and can develop our own enthusiasm for a future that doesn't include us in exactly the same way. We sometimes think of legacy as the part of us that will live on when we leave, but it can also look like loving a new direction enough to set it free to fly.

If we can appreciate the skills and talents required for that aspirational future, we can focus in the present on actively **cultivating** people's gifts and giving them room to develop ways of being and leading that are different from those that made us successful. This fosters trust, empowers in-the-moment leadership, and builds resilience for the future.

As we've seen throughout this book, however, systems are built to persist. One of the most powerful moves a leader can make to steward a new future into being is **championing** both the people and the processes that will shape those tomorrows. Serving as a steady reminder that, yes, a new way is possible gives individuals permission to push the envelope and loosens the grip of institutional habits.

All these moves are in the service of promoting **excellence** in ways that might look a little different because, unless we aspire to a future that looks like yesterday, we must evolve notions of what great looks like. That means reimagining what we measure and ensuring that our tools of evaluation are pointed at what we profess to value.

Doing this well means keeping **equity** front of mind so that we don't inadvertently replicate old patterns by including the same voices and experiences. Breakthrough leaders have an opportunity to tip the scales by examining where bias and disparities have skewed today's systems and proactively exploring alternatives.

It might seem like ensuring *diversity* of background, identity, and perspective is sufficiently implied in the moves itemized above, but many of our institutions still pull for homogeneity, compliance, or adherence to rules and norms that may no longer serve us. Changing those habits and patterns will take time, and until then, a final reminder to ask, "Who's missing?" is another tool of transformation.

the KOAN method

SUCCEED Mantra

Building healthy, sustainable systems doesn't happen overnight. This mantra invites us to consider, at any moment, the future we are building and reminds us that success is built over time and in community.

Chapter Seven—Nurture Networks of Relationship

STRATEGIES—Am I working to preserve and replicate the past, or building the future, now?

How can I notice the pull of the past and shift to more constructive solutions?

UNDERSTANDING—Have I explored the future others aspire to enough to help it into being?

Where can I foster inquiry and curiosity over certainty and repetition?

CULTIVATING—What am I doing to nurture people's growth in areas where I am not an expert?

Can I see aptitudes on the team that might help us become who we aspire to be?

CHAMPIONING—Where is encouragement, reassurance, or appreciation needed?

Who might benefit from support? How can I confer social capital?

EXCELLENCE—What will greatness look like in our desired future?

Are we measuring the things we care about in ways that advance a desired future?

EQUITY—Are we being intentional about disrupting bias and reducing disparities?

Where can we include different voices and perspectives to generate fresh solutions?

DIVERSITY—How daring and disruptive are we being? What else might we be missing?

Whose voices, experience, or expertise might be the key to unleashing a breakthrough?

In this section we have explored how connected leaders can transform systems by building *Kind, Open, Adaptive Networks.*

The closing section shows us what becomes possible when we do.

Thread by thread fabric is made.
Heart by heart community is made.
Star by star the sky is made.
Shoulder to shoulder the world is made.
The power of one is the power of all,
Wilderness is another name for divisionism.
When we are together, we are civilized,
Civilization is synonym for nonsectarianism.
But the tragedy of the world is,
Each thread thinks they are all important.
And the problems faced by others,
Are all considered insignificant.
A world where callousness is assumed cool,
Is but a billion-dollar grave of the fool.[138]

~Abhijit Naskar

Building a Common Good

It is easy to point outside ourselves at lies and deceptions, from "fake news" to political propaganda to conspiracy theories and bemoan their effect on our ability to get good things done together. It is much harder to look in the mirror and ask where we might be deluding ourselves—where we have succumbed to self-righteousness or accepted impartial but palatable answers to complex questions. We are living in exciting, if fraught, times. We've got real challenges to solve, but also more resources and a window of opportunity that make this moment especially potent.

We have developed technology that can connect people and their ideas across time and space. We can gather and analyze huge volumes of data in ways that were completely out of reach to the average person even a decade ago. We are also benefiting from a little inflection point in history brought about by the biological, ecological, political, and social disruptions happening around the world in the early 2020s. Swift changes to manner and means of work and massive changes to entire industries and communities have loosened our grip on a sense of what must be, giving us a chance to reimagine and rewrite this next chapter in human history.

The early 2020s saw social and organizational change on an unprecedented scale, all at once, and across the globe. In effect, the whole world participated in a massive unplanned, real-time experiment in systems change at nearly every societal level in every institution and organization. While disruptive and devastating for many, this inflection point also gave us an opportunity to call into question the many taken-for-granteds of the last era of human evolution and growth.

Throughout the early months of 2020, scientists were struggling to understand this novel virus, to find how it was transmitted, how it worked on the body, and finally how to come up with treatments and, ultimately, a vaccine, faster than had ever been done before. They were doing this without widespread or coordinated testing efforts, and with incomplete and suspicious data sets. The environment in which they were working and giving advice was highly politicized from the outset and filled with misinformation and opportunists.

The biological threat would prove easier to understand and solve than the social one.

Different countries experienced this time in varying ways and degrees, but the impact was global in a way few other events have ever been. As the disparities in death rates across marginalized and vulnerable populations became glaringly obvious, it also created a global reckoning as many asked what else might not be quite as it seemed.

Businesses of all sizes, in fact whole industries, were confronting their own turbulence and many struggled to survive. Governmental, corporate, and personal debt mounted rapidly from already high levels. The infrastructure weaknesses in many societies were stark and endlessly deferred maintenance began to catch up with us.

Globalization showed us its ugliest side as international travel and trade accelerated both the transmission of the disease and fueled its evolution, making effective treatments a moving target. Those same systems and industries began to crumble as disruptions impacted everything up and down the supply chain, affecting the cost and availability of a wide range of consumer goods and services.

The need to isolate in order to reduce the contagion launched a social change process, a set of social experiments really, that immediately altered how many people lived and worked. Where it could, schooling and work became virtual at lightning speed. In communities and industries where physical distancing was impossible or impractical, the virus spread, and jobs and lives were lost in record numbers. The disproportionate impact on the poor and already socially disadvantaged brought pre-existing disparities into glaring relief. The breach in the social contract was laid bare in plain sight.

This was something of a pulling back of the veil on all manner of social challenges.

Access to quality health care and treatment was clearly not equitable—either within countries or across the global community. Our methods of handling everything from homelessness to incarceration to mental and behavioral health crumbled under pandemic conditions. Gross systemic inequities in policing and law enforcement came into even sharper relief. The intersections between voting, reproductive, and gun rights all converged in clearly interdependent yet hard-to-parse ways.

The ways race-based (dis)advantage has been baked into laws and policies and systems have found space for public conversation around how to create more Just, Equitable, Diverse, and Inclusive (JEDI) spaces, and have also been met with resistance, reluctance, and fear. Competing world views are battling for supremacy.

If we pause to look at any of these issues, it is clear that none of them are simple either/or questions and that devising truly common-good solutions requires breakthrough thinking. Win-lose solutions are untenable, but we haven't yet learned to co-create well together across our differences.

The consequences of the COVID-19 pandemic in our collective history will not be fully known for many years to come, but already we can see both the massive impacts that pre-existing structural disparities have had on individual and group experiences and the unique opportunity afforded us by a moment in time that inherently calls long-held assumptions into question. We can see that many structures, and the political and economic philosophies that helped fuel industrial growth in the 20th century, became increasingly brittle under the pressures of intensely rapid change—offices and conferences, assembly lines and supply chains, and all manner of performance management systems became irrelevant overnight.

In some cases, those things we once believed kept us connected and efficient served to accelerate the spread of a virulent disease as it raced across the globe and disrupted life in big and small ways worldwide. Of course, the last century was rife with all manner of social upheaval—the first half plagued by vicious wars and the development of new forms of militarism, and the latter half characterized by various attempts at massive social planning, deregulation of economies, and the rise of globalization. In its closing decade, the propagation of the internet and its attendant effects on life and work also connected us more intimately and rapidly than ever before and revealed persistent global conflicts and dramatic effects of climate change that, often first and disproportionately, affect the poorest among us.

In this context, there is both a lot of incentive and a unique opportunity to fundamentally redefine the systems that structure and govern our lives. How governance works both locally and globally, and how we organize to solve problems from our local neighborhoods to the largest megacorporations, must evolve and adapt to the complexity of our times. Clearly and painfully, some of our ways of working and living have directly contributed to the scope and scale of this crisis, and we have little desire to go back to outmoded solutions.

The old adage that one can never go home again rings especially true in this context. For many, "home" wasn't so great to begin with and we have a real opportunity to build back better.

Hybrid work, in some form, is likely here to stay. Conferences, concerts, and sporting events may look oddly different for better and for worse. How families and communities gather, celebrate, and organize has been reimagined. These are the moments that hold potential for true shifts in understanding, but only if we meet the moment. Each institution and organization will be adapting in its own ways—some with more intention, positive growth, and success than others. Those that lead the way will have learned to master the art of meeting division with curiosity and interest to unleash the kinds of discovery that will produce real breakthroughs.

Chapter Eight

The Future is Already Here

Exploration is the engine that drives innovation. Innovation drives economic growth.

~Edith Widder

The KOAN method gives us a framework and mindset from which to engage persistent and pernicious challenges in new ways. Where it was once easier to see many of our social challenges as local or discrete, we can now see more clearly that we have built systems that no longer serve us. Decades of research shows that alternatives do exist, and we've seen many examples of people, organizations, and communities experimenting with new models in exciting ways, and to great effect.

For many years, individual leaders have gotten the message that empathy and trust are important for team building, that empowering people with the information they need to do their jobs saves money and speeds success, that agile organizations are more desirable than rigid and inflexible ones, and that collaboration across boundaries of all kinds is good for business. This emphasis on individual competencies and attributes, however, has largely masked the persistence of systems that make those models hard to implement and that are still too often at odds with how we measure success.

When Sheryl Sandberg, then COO of Facebook (and later Meta), first advocated that women "lean in" to opportunities at work, she was at once hailed for her brand of DIY feminism that put agency in the hands of female leaders and chided for ignoring the many ways in which no measure of sticking one's neck out could overcome the interlocking systems of education, acculturation, hiring, and promotion that still distributed power in wildly uneven ways across gender lines.[139]

The drive and desire to build something new is not what is lacking. The will to look at what is keeping us stuck and remove barriers is what has been in shorter supply. While the thought of a start-from-scratch do-over might be daunting, the truth is that the future is already here, in pockets, and **the KOAN method** shows us how we can foster its flourishing more broadly.

The opportunity in front of us is palpable—the innovation required to solve the most pressing challenges of our time requires us to think together in new ways. We can see that old systems are serving us poorly in this ever more interconnected world.

Old strategies of building walls and beating one another into submission don't work for solving these problems. We need the creativity and perspective of people looking at challenges from different angles to create the level of breakthroughs necessary to heal the brokenness of our systems and communities.

Making this shift will take intentionality. We've created a well-worn groove in the habit of characterizing differences as things to be managed, avoided, or overcome. There are both social and biological reasons for this, but evidence of the ineffectiveness of this strategy is all around us.

Yet we can still deceive ourselves into believing the rightness of our narrow positions at the expense of cultivating collective wisdom.

Throughout this book, I have used art, poetry, and other forms of creative writing to "loosen up" otherwise rigid or fixed thinking in ways that, I hope, have allowed you to explore new ideas and break the hold of well-worn beliefs. Opportunities to challenge our own thinking are all around us.

Throughout this book, we explored time-tested research and concrete business cases alongside these pieces of poetry and a collection of mantras whose purpose was to both illuminate an idea and disrupt stuck thinking.

We learned to listen in new ways to the stirrings that signal untapped potential. As we go about our lives and consider the spheres of leadership and influence that we operate from, it is helpful to remember that the future needs us to be connected enough to overcome our divisions.

No matter what side of any given divide we are on, if it feels in our best interest to come out on top, to withhold information we think might give someone else the upper hand, to impose rules or policies that favor my side at your expense, or to close ranks, we will continue to build all manner of silos or border walls to keep the great divide alive, and solutions that serve us all will remain elusive.

If, on the other hand, we can put our own ideas or opinions aside, just for a moment, and genuinely listen, we might find that there is some sense in what others have to say, or that a perspective someone else already has is the missing piece of the equation we haven't been able to solve on our own. This doesn't mean that we abandon our principles or history or people. Quite the opposite. It means that we recognize that we're all in this together and that if we aren't finding solutions that are good for everyone, we're most likely making things worse.

The problem with being polarized is not that poles exist—it's that we think one "side" is meant to prevail and that there is supposed to be a winner. We have learned to want to win, and definitely to not want to lose, so we defend what we know, even if we don't like it all that much.

One of the most important things for us to grapple with, in reimagining systems that create real breakthroughs and help us develop common-good solutions, is how we set our routines and practices up to deal with differences so that they are less likely to devolve into division and are better suited to producing truly breakthrough discoveries.

We saw that social change outfits, like Ashoka, and innovation platforms, like Open IDEO, are helping people to discover and implement high-impact ideas all around the world. We learned how collaboratives like Coralus and The Carbon Almanac are harnessing the power of connection to fuel entrepreneurial innovation and address the world's most pressing problems. And we saw how multinational companies like Unilever are building resilience into their systems by tapping the creative power of their networks to solve challenges faster and better.

The principles that **the KOAN method** is based on are time-tested and proven. Adopting them begins from remembering that we are all in this together. From wherever you are, right in this moment, ask yourself where you might be the source of a breakthrough waiting to happen.

Where might a little more empathy, or more transparency, or greater flexibility, or a broader view of the community of affected parties, create just the shift that the moment calls for?

Chapter Nine

In it Together

When we drop fear, we can draw nearer to people.

~bell hooks

The real lesson from my many sojourns into the desert, and all the other journeys I've taken into myself, has been the realization that none of us are ever alone in our endeavors, and it is always the illusion of separation that keeps us stuck and at odds with each other.

Writing this book has been an exercise in alchemy for me—in taking the seeds of ideas and a lifetime of learning and experience and weaving them into something coherent and whole. As I've laid down each word and chosen examples to share, I've been reminded of how far I've come and what the road I have traveled has taught me.

I have so often been right up close with the feeling of loneliness in my life, for having so often had to start over and leave behind something I'd come to love or that had become familiar. There have been many solitary moments during this period of writing, too, but it has also reminded me, maybe even helped me, to fully embody in a way I hadn't quite yet, that I have never ever been alone.

I've long been a fan of the saying, "If you wish to go fast, go alone. To go far, find your way together." Versions of this have been attributed as an African proverb as well as to a whole range of authors, intellectuals, and business leaders. I rarely see it quoted exactly the same way and, for me, that is partially the point: When we make sense of things in community, how we understand them evolves.

Over time I've also become less of a fan of the first part of the phrase because I don't actually believe anymore that where we end up can be the same if we go it alone. Traveling together inherently shapes us, affects what we see and how we make sense of it, and helps us to arrive at an altogether different place—wiser and transformed by the journey.

As I was putting the finishing touches on this book, I could palpably feel how each lesson, insight, and mantra had been shaped, polished, and refined over years of conversations with hundreds of people. Sometimes I remembered exactly where the seed of an idea was planted or traced the roots of a principle back to a specific person or experience.

Other times, I felt like the concept itself was ageless and had always been with me in some form but was coming into sharper relief in a valuable new way. Here I was at one moment, writing alone while simultaneously feeling a responsibility to do right by (and for) everyone who had shaped me and this work.

The same week that I finished the first complete draft of this manuscript, I came across a video from just a few years earlier that made me smile from ear to ear with the memory.

I've reflected on the way it touched me and how it underscored the importance of this work for me like this:

February 2023
Boulder, CO

The afternoon light was streaming through the big windows in my living room as I looked for something on my laptop. I was excited for the evolution we were putting in place on my team that would begin to shift power to the center of our organization at Integrated Work, empowering the next generation of leaders to live and lead **the KOAN method** *in practice.*

As I looked for the place to put some resources for this newly formed team, I stumbled on something I had both forgotten about completely and which, I could tell, had been with me all along.

The file name caught my eye first: "Next Stage Orientation.mp4"

Then I noticed the date: July 2019

It felt both like such a long time ago, and only yesterday.

Smiling, I clicked on the words and my media player sprang to life.

the KOAN method

There, on my screen, was my dear friend, trusted colleague, and partner in all of this, Dianne Dickerson, setting the stage for a new way of working that we were just beginning to try out. She and I had been talking about and experimenting with new models of organizing for some time—reading up on models like holacracy[140] and sociocracy,[141] going to training programs, and experimenting with tools and techniques, seeing what we could learn from others who were also working to forge new paths.

I was immediately struck by her presence—how warm and connected she felt even from a distance, all the while talking about fairly technical things—and remembered how our partnership was first formed.

I remembered how she'd joined me at a conference in Aspen, Colorado, back in 2011. Effectively sent to supervise and chaperone me when we both worked inside a system where trust was hard won. How we'd sat together over breakfast in Arizona many years later, preparing for a day of systems-scale environmental work and feeling like, just maybe, we were on the cusp of being able to put approaches we'd long believed in into practice. I marveled at how the vision we shared for a new way of leading and organizing that we'd been exploring together for years was coming to fruition.

Sitting in my sunny living room, Dianne's voice coming to me through the computer reminded me that **the KOAN method** was really born out of the regular practice of leaning into curiosity in the face of difference, over and over again.

As she talked about the "softer around the edges" approach to other models of self-organizing, she and her colleague Melissa referred to "Next Stage Organization," and I could feel how important her friendship had been, how critical the dozens of times we had brought each other back to our more grounded and connected selves had been in enabling us both to bring a little more kindness to our daily leadership.

I laughed when I saw the Aaron Dignan quote she'd included to help our team consider the work involved in systems change, "I'd rather change the aquarium than change the fish." I wondered how many times we'd changed the water in our growing aquarium by then and realized that I no longer wished for a time when we would be "done." Adapting to changing conditions felt so much more natural than standing still while the world moved now.

When she compared the potential of self-organizing and self-managing systems to the murmuration of birds, I paused and went to find a few of my favorite videos of this phenomenon online.[142,143,144] I wasn't sure we were quite there yet but could feel the potential emerging that a whole group could coordinate its activities by paying close attention to the handful of people closest to them, ensuring the whole held together and moved in a shared direction.

There were always people around us with whom we could connect and coordinate to make a meaningful difference. The idea that people far away from us were more or less important to the success of the whole was an illusion. That illusion could stop us from paying attention to what we were sensing in the moment and have us miss what we could do about it from wherever we were.

As Dianne's soothing and steady voice carried me on, I looked up from the couch and across the room into my office, at the portraits of women that hung on the wall behind my desk. To anyone who asked, I called these women "The Ladies Who Have My Back."

Long before COVID made videoconferencing commonplace, I spent a lot of time on my computer, taking calls with clients all over the world, and had been very intentional in choosing artwork that meant something to me. I discovered Meg, a fellow female entrepreneur and artist, online and handpicked a collection of portraits from her "feminist icons"[145] series, hanging them so that they were always over my shoulders while I worked.

Each of the women I selected had taught me something about courage and care, and the hard work and perseverance required to make any lasting change by example, and in their own way. Some I'd admired for a long time and had encountered early in life—their examples having shaped and influenced me for decades. Others were either younger than or newer to me, but also significant. Knowing that they were constantly behind me while I met with colleagues and clients reminded me every day that none of us gets here alone, and that anyone who arrives anywhere is also given the opportunity to hold the door open for others.

They also remind me that no human is perfect and that none of us will ever get to solve all of the challenges we might hope to in our lifetimes. Being perfect isn't the point. Taking the first step and then the next one is. Our job is not to finish, but to begin.

The beauty of this is that to begin, we don't need to know exactly how the story will end or be certain of success. My attention came back to the screen and Dianne as the video drew to a close. She reminded me of a phrase we hadn't used in a while but that served as a reminder that some things ought not be forced, and that there is always a "last responsible moment" to do something that both encourages real presence and attunement to what each moment calls for and allows us to move at speed, together.

I looked out the window and noticed the light had shifted as the sun began to fall behind the mountains. A milestone birthday was coming up and I was heading to the beach where I'd spent my youth, looking forward to watching the sun set over the ocean as I was prepared to close a circle with so much power and meaning.

On the one hand, I could feel the weight of decades that had passed and of all the time I'd traveled since then; and on the other, I could see so clearly how that road had shaped me. I thought about the dozens of women I'd befriended through the Generative Council, and the connections I'd made through Emerging Women's Power Circles, and about all of the Amazing Ladies (both official and honorary) in my life.

I thought of the people who had reminded me that I'm a poet at heart and appreciated that part of myself enough to encourage it to emerge in a form that might be valuable to others.

I marveled that I truly had friends all over the world who now seemed to show up and boomerang back in, at just the right moments, despite months and years passing between us. I thought of the colleagues and clients and teachers and mentors and students and team members I'd worked with, all of whom had shaped this network of thinking and doing and being in the world.

I was pretty sure I wouldn't have gotten it done in the same way without Dianne!

If I had forged ahead alone, I would have arrived in an entirely different place.

As I shifted my attention back to what I'd gone looking for on my computer in the first place, I was reminded of a poem I wrote at a time when my whole life felt like a roller coaster and I couldn't have controlled the ride if I tried.

And now, here I was, arriving somewhere I hoped would make a difference, at a turn in the road that felt both like it had been a lifetime coming, and was arriving just in time, at exactly the right moment.

I felt ready, and like just maybe the world was too.

Poetic Pause
Universe at the Wheel

January 6, 2021

When you finally allow
The Universe to take the wheel
Everything lightens,
Suddenly.

It feels like homecoming, really,
As you remember, again,
That you never
Knew where you were going.

Were always being guided,
Only you had forgotten to listen;
Kept trying to chart your own course . . .
Decide your own ends.

In every moment
That you remember
To let go
And be steered by the Almighty,

Whatever that is,
(And there will be many rememberings
Because forgetting is so easy)
You land, in the present,

Exactly where you are meant to be,
Already completely on course,
Despite your best attempts
At getting lost along the way

Chapter Ten

Leading the Way

We are a part of everything that is beneath us, above us, and around us. Our past is our present, our present is our future, and our future is seven generations past and present.

~Winona LaDuke

What is the future we want to build?

The way we have organized human activity in the name of progress has shifted many times over tens of thousands of years, with change generally prompted by the need to accomplish something new that old ways were poorly suited to. We're at one of those inflection points again now.

Somewhere along the line, basic human kindness got branded as "unprofessional," and generations of employees and leaders have learned to behave in ways that drive emotions underground rather than learning to accept, integrate, and navigate them well.[146] Leaders, boards, and investors allowed themselves to believe that treating employees like whole people, providing a living wage, or offering generous benefits, was at odds with being profitable. So, we started managing human beings like resources and, instead, invested trillions of dollars in management technologies designed to turn people into profit.

The reasons for doing things the old way don't necessarily exist anymore. The global workforce is more educated than ever, the internet provides access to more information than any one human can process, and the problems that groups of people need to solve often spill over the boundaries of any one organization or group.

Today's problems are too complex to solve in isolation, and a divide-and-conquer strategy is poorly suited to a deeply interconnected world.

Yet, the world FEELS more divided than ever—full of friction and conflict and large-scale existential threats. History, culture, and biology have primed us to attack or avoid things that aren't familiar or don't make sense. What was adaptive for survival thousands of years ago, however, is poorly suited to the dynamic, ever-changing, and highly networked world we now live in.

What if that moment of friction or frustration when tensions seem at their highest were the very moment when the breakthrough was closest at hand?

If we are up to the task and ready to answer Buckminster Fuller's call to "build a new model that makes the existing model obsolete," we can't look only at the actions of individuals. We have to look at the ways in which we build systems that reward, celebrate, and elevate some ideas at the expense of others and ask whether those are the solutions that best serve us in discovering common good solutions.

Change has begun. It is ours to build.

That is the spirit behind the KOAN concept: if we can stay in the discomfort of uncertainty and not-knowing long enough, and with enough curiosity, breakthroughs will find us.

That means that the challenges we face require divergent thinking to solve and the once-adaptive "fight-flee-freeze-fawn" response is now an act of self-sabotage, tripping us up, keeping us reactive rather than responsive, and getting in the way of achieving the positive progress and outcomes we want and need.

It turns out that most of the challenges that humans face aren't that different from organization to organization and community to community. In all cases, meeting uncertainty with curiosity is the birthplace of innovation, so we've explored how to leverage *the KOAN method* to get big things done together in a dynamic world:

Be Kind: Listen and act empathetically, meet differences with real curiosity;

Be Open: Trust people with information that impacts their lives and work and be open to feedback;

Be Adaptive: Develop systems that are resilient and agile; and

Build a Network: Recognize our interdependence and lean into the partnerships that will produce innovation.

the KOAN method

Today's biggest challenges can't be solved by doubling down on the strategies that created them and none of us can see all the facets from all the angles necessary to come up with truly novel ideas.

In Zen Buddhism, a koan is a riddle or a paradox that helps us remember that all stories and explanations are partial and incomplete. There isn't a right answer to a koan, but if we sit with the questions long enough, our grip on what we believe to be true tends to loosen just enough for new insights to emerge.

Solving today's biggest challenges requires this kind of openness to discovery as we work to build a flourishing future where more people can thrive more often.

The how-to manual for this new way of mobilizing people to do great work together hasn't been written yet, and that's as it should be. (After all, a policy manual on how to ditch the policy manual might be the epitome of paradox!)

Nevertheless, I hope that the principles outlined here will inspire leaders to move beyond individual or interpersonal changes and take a meaningful look, alongside their team members, at how they organize.

I believe the principles outlined here can help us navigate this paradox at work by inspiring us to *live into the promise of the KOAN method by building Kind, Open, Adaptive Networks* of people working together to reach shared goals.

A KOAN Case Study: Leading into the Future

Even with all of these resources and examples, the scale of change can feel daunting, but for anyone inspired by the possibility of a new way, the good news is that there are already others leading the way. Many courageous souls have gone first already and there are networks to join and models to point to as we each contribute to charting new possibilities.

In 2006, B Lab was founded by a group of friends who, after achieving "success" by traditional measures and selling their start-up to a larger conglomerate, wanted to create a vehicle to certify and hold companies publicly accountable for the ways they "benefitted workers, communities, the environment, and customers."[147] They believed that one of the biggest ways in which systems are stuck is in the primacy placed on shareholder returns in many large companies. This drive to achieve a particular kind of profitability on very short timescales virtually demands short-term maneuvering at the expense of more thoughtful or holistic solutions that might be of greater benefit to the common good in the long term.

Since then, thousands of B Corps have been certified all over the world—amending their operating agreements to place people and the planet, alongside profit, as a business driver, and creating conditions for leaders and organizations of all kinds to reimagine how to build systems that create positive impacts to that triple bottom line. As the network has grown, so has their potential for impact.

Being a B Corp is more than just a seal of approval, it's a signal to employees, customers, and potential partners of all kinds that one is committed to walking the talk. It's also a membership in a growing community of like-minded leaders who are all actively reimagining everything from supply chains to employee benefits to organizing models every day.

It's a crucible of innovation for reimagining the future of work.

While there are lots of B Corps of all sizes, those who are bigger and more well-known are also leveraging the platform to push the creative envelope even further.

Patagonia is one extreme example of what is possible when we throw out the old playbook and adopt an anything-is-possible stance. Founder and longtime CEO, Yvon Chouinard, was long fond of saying that he never intended to be a businessman, having gotten his start making climbing gear for himself and his friends in a workshop. From its earliest days, the company stood out for nontraditional work practices like encouraging staff to drop work when the surf was up and treating work like play.

Over the years, as the climate impacts on the natural environment that Patagonia employees and customers most loved to play in became more and more apparent, they centered their purpose on saving our home planet by donating 1% of all proceeds to charitable causes and becoming both a certified B Corp and a California benefit corporation. Then, in 2022, Chouinard went even further by declaring that "the Earth is now our only shareholder" and donating 100% of the company's voting stock to the newly founded Patagonia Purpose Trust, while all nonvoting stock was given to the Holdfast Collective, "a nonprofit dedicated to fighting the environmental crisis and defending nature."[148]

In making this announcement, Chouinard declared "Truth be told, there were no good options available. So, we created our own."

Every day there are new examples of breakthrough leaders looking beyond the divisions we've taken for granted for too long to imagine new ways of leading and organizing.

At Integrated Work, we've been experimenting with *the KOAN method* for several years now, taking the best of what we have each learned from successes and setbacks both here and in all of the other places our talented and diverse team have worked at, led, and contributed to over the years.

We've partnered with clients to help them reimagine new futures and learned from their ingenuity along the way. Every day we experience ways in which old impulses to divide, segment, and silo interfere with the future we are trying to build and help hold one another to account for not staying stuck there long.

As we look at how to continue evolving our organizations to meet the challenges of a rapidly changing world, we invite other mission-driven leaders to join us in building a more inclusive world where human-first principles and a commitment to transparency and curiosity fuel our ability to amplify our impact, together.

KOAN Mantra

Existing systems were built to persist but are often poorly suited to the futures we want to build. This mantra reminds us that a different set of options is available and gives us the tools to build new tomorrows together.

Chapter Ten—Leading the Way

cultivate **kind** cultures

foster **open** systems

be **adaptive**

nurture **networks**
of relationship

Am I operating from empathy and curiosity and treating everyone with dignity?

Am I protecting something that could be shared or extending and inviting trust?

Where can I be more flexible or help the system be more resilient?

What can I do to build stronger connections today?

Chapter Ten—Leading the Way

Thank you for the gift of your attention. We hope you'll join us at *koanmethod.com* to dive deeper into the resources we've referenced here and explore how you can be a part of the movement to put **the KOAN method** into practice.

We can't wait to learn what you are already doing to build common good futures that benefit us all.

KOAN Mantras

HIKE Mantra

CARE Mantra

HEAL Mantra

TRUST Mantra

VIABLE Mantra

BREATH Mantra

JEDI Mantra

SUCCEED Mantra

KOAN Mantra

the KOAN method

HIKE Mantra

Feeling stuck or holding on to a solution that just isn't working is an indication that certainty is interfering with curiosity. This mantra reminds us that no matter where we are in a learning journey, there is always a first or next step to take.

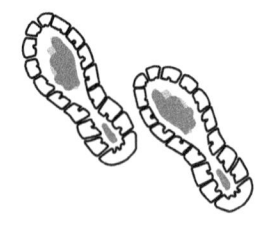

KOAN Mantras

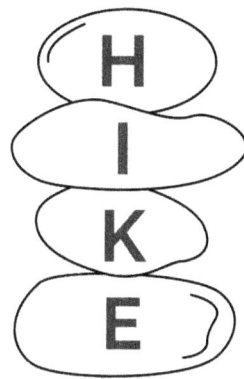

Where is *HUBRIS* holding
me back?

How can I bring more *HUMILITY*
to this question or challenge?

What *INSIGHTS* are
challenging my old beliefs?

Where else can I be in
intentional *INQUIRY* around
this issue or question?

What new *KNOWLEDGE*
am I acquiring; how is it
changing me?

What *KINSHIP* do I feel with
this issue; how am I already
a part of it?

What does it look and
feel like to be *EFFECTIVE*
in this work?

How can I be more *EMBODIED*
around this question;
who lives this well?

CARE Mantra

When creativity is low and tensions are high, it is an indicator that a group or team is on edge. This mantra helps us explore strategies to shift from reactivity to creativity by creating the containers of CARE that support psychological safety.

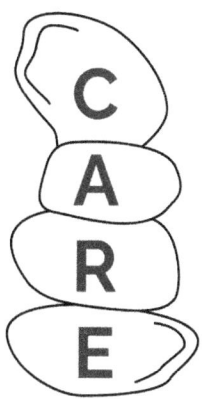

How can I foster
deeper *CONNECTION?*

What needs
AFFIRMATION here?

Are my interactions
helping or hindering?

Who needs to feel
seen or heard?

What will support
physical and emotional
REGULATION?

What support
can I provide?

Where is *EMPOWERMENT*
flourishing?

Where is it not? What is
my role in fostering it?

the KOAN method

HEAL Mantra

Organizations, systems, and communities have legacies that can keep us mired in old patterns. This mantra helps us explore the past with curiosity and care so that we can build a better tomorrow.

KOAN Mantras

HISTORY – What paths have we walked (personally, organizationally) to arrive here?

Who has benefited? Who has been harmed? What more is there for me to learn? How can I connect?

EMPATHY – How can we cultivate caring curiosity in the face of stories and experiences different from our own?

Are there things we need to mourn or grieve? Are there things to celebrate? How can I affirm the collective experience?

ACTION – Knowing what we now know, what new steps can we see to take?

What meaningful actions can we take in service of a better tomorrow? How will we resource ourselves for the journey?

LEADERSHIP – What qualities will be needed to get us where we want to go?

What paths will this leader have walked? What resources or support will they need? How can I empower their contribution?

TRUST Mantra

When secrecy and withholding are present, leaders risk not receiving critical information in a timely way. This mantra helps us identify where breakdowns may exist and build foundations of mutual trust and transparency.

KOAN Mantras

TELL the truth

What can you share?
When privacy is required,
can you offer explanations
or provide helpful context?

RESPECT everyone

Are you treating all perspectives
as valid and all people
with dignity? How do you
demonstrate this?

UNDERSTAND yourself

Do you know your triggers?
What helps you recognize
your biases? How do you
live your values?

SHOW up

Do people expect you to follow
through and be dependable?
Does your intent match
your impact?

TAKE responsibility

When you make a mistake,
do you own it and make it right?
Where can you take
100% responsibility?

VIABLE Mantra

Having a clear direction and shared commitments inspires groups of people to co-create exciting new futures. This mantra helps us set a course together and define how we want to show up on the way and sets key milestones for progress. True agility comes from faith that we can adjust our course in the face of challenges.

This mantra helps us proactively predict what might interfere with progress and cultivate a learning mindset that strengthens creativity to keep us moving in the direction of our goals, even as the world shifts around us.

KOAN Mantras

Is your *VISION* clear and compelling?

Does your team know where they are headed, and are they inspired to get there?

Have you articulated *IDEALS* that will inform choices and guide behavior?

Are you clear about how you want to show up and how your behaviors will influence outcomes?

Do you have an *APPROACH* that is well-defined and broadly understood?

What milestones will serve as guideposts and help you stay the course in dynamic conditions?

What *BARRIERS* might get in your way; how might you overcome them?

Can you get as good at generating solutions as at predicting setbacks?

Have you identified *LESSONS* that will help you turn setbacks into successes?

What capacity do you need to build, or insights do you need to succeed?

What methods of *EVALUATION* will allow you to gather feedback and adapt?

Are you measuring the things that matter most to your desired outcomes?

BREATH Mantra

When we are distracted or dislocated, our "best selves" are often out of reach. This mantra reminds us that there are many paths back to presence and gives us options, at any moment, for returning to the now.

KOAN Mantras

Am I *BEING* the change I wish to create?

What mode of *REFLECTION* suits me best?

How can I *EXERCISE* to energize?

What *ASPIRATION* keeps me inspired and motivated?

Am I spending my *TIME* on what matters most?

Is my *HEART* leading the way? Am I listening?

the KOAN method

JEDI Mantra

No "great" solutions work for only some of the people, some of the time. This mantra keeps us present to places where inequity might interfere with optimal outcomes and helps us explore what real breakthroughs require.

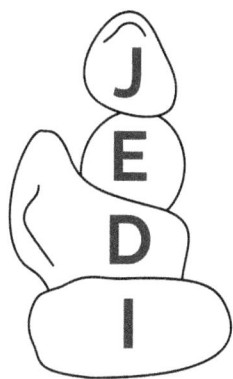

JUSTICE—Does the "how and what" of decisions and actions foster flourishing?

Will more people be better off as a result of these decisions?

EQUITY—Does the action we are taking ensure opportunity is evenly distributed?

Are we working proactively to redress past harms or disparities?

DIVERSITY—Are we attending to the full range of identities and histories held by people within a setting?

Whose perspectives and experiences might yield fresh insight or get us unstuck?

INCLUSION—Are we conscious of how a diverse range of people are represented in processes prior to actions and outcomes?

Is everyone valued for their contributions? Do they feel safe to bring ideas forward?

the KOAN method

SUCCEED Mantra

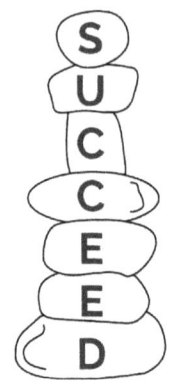

Building healthy, sustainable systems doesn't happen overnight. This mantra invites us to consider, at any moment, the future we are building and reminds us that success is built over time and in community.

KOAN Mantras

STRATEGIES—Am I working to preserve and replicate the past, or building the future, now?

How can I notice the pull of the past and shift to more constructive solutions?

UNDERSTANDING—Have I explored the future others aspire to enough to help it into being?

Where can I foster inquiry and curiosity over certainty and repetition?

CULTIVATING—What am I doing to nurture people's growth in areas where I am not an expert?

Can I see aptitudes on the team that might help us become who we aspire to be?

CHAMPIONING—Where is encouragement, reassurance, or appreciation needed?

Who might benefit from support? How can I confer social capital?

EXCELLENCE—What will greatness
look like in our desired future?

Are we measuring the things we care about in ways that advance a desired future?

EQUITY—Are we being intentional about disrupting bias and reducing disparities?

Where can we include different voices and perspectives to generate fresh solutions?

DIVERSITY—How daring and disruptive are we being?
What else might we be missing?

Whose voices, experience, or expertise might be the key to unleashing a breakthrough?

KOAN Mantra

Existing systems were built to persist but are often poorly suited to the futures we want to build. This mantra reminds us that a different set of options is available and gives us the tools to build new tomorrows together.

KOAN Mantras

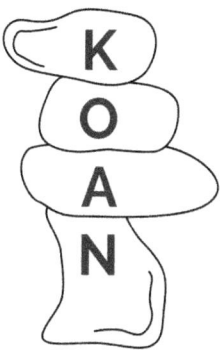

cultivate **kind** cultures

foster **open** systems

be **adaptive**

nurture **networks**
of relationship

Am I operating from empathy and curiosity and treating everyone with dignity?

Am I protecting something that could be shared or extending and inviting trust?

Where can I be more flexlble or help the system be more resilient?

What can I do to build stronger connections today?

Like good science, the resolution of a koan requires a trust in the larger pattern which underlies the happening that the mind does not understand, and the understanding which is gained is often accompanied by a deep appreciation of the elegance of that pattern, the intelligence of the nature of things.

A sense of wonder.

An appreciation of the very mystery which has frustrated us.

A sense of belonging to it.[149]

~Rachel Naomi Remen

Gratitude

The journey that produced this book has been walked in community over a lifetime. It is the result of both support and struggle.

I am grateful to everyone whose influence affected me in ways that allowed this work to emerge and the challenge of acknowledging some of them is that others are inevitably not named. There are far too many "invisible hands" to recite so I'll just thank a few of you here:

My parents for raising me in a "bigger than me" world from the beginning.

My children for expanding it yet again and putting it all in perspective.

My brother for being my biggest champion, even when I didn't deserve it.

My many clients and colleagues for so many influential experiences.

My Generative Council sisters for reconnecting me to myself and to the land.

My community of Amazing Ladies for so much kindness, presence, and care.

And special thanks are due to:

Chaz for bearing with me as we both grew up and for raising two great kids.

Melissa and Jeff for showing me the joys of lifelong friendship.

Stan for believing in and pushing my thinking over the years.

Brenda for saying "yes" and shaping the course of my work in the world.

Ron and Elease for helping me take flight.

Trent for being a lifelong JEDI-Journeyer with me.

Chantal for inspiring and supporting my emergence in so many ways.

Vicki for helping me be brave enough to build new models without a map.

Cheryl for being the most magical friend a girl could want.

Everyone at Integrated Work for being *in it* with me, daily.

Allison and my Sofia Sisters for expanding my capacity to steward this vision.

Jessica for trusting me to build on what she began, even when it was hard.

Seth for being the kind of supportive, generative leader I aspire to be daily.

Kate for helping me to see the future I want to build (and everything, really).

Nick for his amazing design sensibility and bringing the spirit of the text alive.

The Publish Your Purpose team who helped me get it all done, beautifully.

Emma for a lifetime of friendship on a road full of twists and turns.

Catherine for the gift of connection, community, and the best birthday ever!

Dianne for being a true friend, inspiring thought partner, and mystic muse.

And to Alex, for showing up in just the right ways at just the right times to point me in the direction of my best self. You have helped to make me both a better writer and a kinder, bolder, and more wholehearted human.

Thank you.

About the Author

Jennifer Lyn Simpson, PhD (she/her) is Integrated Work's CEO. She developed **the KOAN method** based on over 30 years of experience working in and with organizations across the academic, private, public, corporate, and not-for-profit sectors to create more meaningful and effective ways of living and working together across differences.

She is an author, artist, entrepreneur, and idealist whose vision includes the integration of creativity and personal inquiry as catalysts for individual and collective transformation.

She holds a Bachelor's degree from Syracuse University, a Masters and Doctorate from the University of Colorado at Boulder and continues her own learning and development by regularly participating in immersive experiential leadership, contemplative, nature-based, and JEDI programs.

She still teaches University classes, works with executives committed to evolving their organizations to meet a changing world, and develops and delivers transformational experiences that help people amplify their impact by being more human, together.

When she isn't working with mission-driven leaders to amplify their impact, leading her team, or enjoying time with her growing children, she explores life's persistent questions through art, poetry, and creative writing, and spending as much time in nature as she can conjure.

About the Business

In 1998, Integrated Work was born out of Jessica Hartung's vision that work and life go together, that a more seamlessly integrated, humane way of leading organizations just might be possible.

A lot has changed since then and as the organization has shifted and evolved over time it has been *learning together along the journey that has made it possible.*

Every step of the way.

Today, Integrated Work remains a woman-owned, woman-led firm devoted to building the leaders our society needs through real-world work. We focus exclusively on mission-driven organizations, and we're fond of working with leaders who are out to create meaningful impact at scale.

We have deep experience and expertise in building high-performing teams, purpose-driven strategic planning, developing leadership content and training curricula on many topics, and providing the kind of thoughtful and engaging facilitation that moves groups to action.

If you are a Breakthrough Leader ready to build the Kind, Open, Adaptive Networks that will unleash the co-creativity necessary to solve today's most pressing problems, Integrated Work can help you find the way.

integratedwork.com

koanmethod.com

This book has attempted to synthesize the work of authors, scholars, artists, poets, activists, visionaries, and change-makers across disciplines and cultures and over the course of centuries.

In many cases, these are people whose work I have admired and immersed myself in over years. In others, I've come across an idea more recently and still feel early in my own full understanding of it.

I don't make any claims to doing that body of work the justice it deserves in these pages but do hope that I've illuminated a binding thread that ties the pieces together in a way that might make all of it even more valuable.

As I've written and edited these pages over the last several months, it's been apparent how quickly ideas grow stale if they don't evolve. We don't live in a world where a point-in-time book can be the end of the conversation or be expected to serve as a reliable reference over many years without a refresh.

the KOAN method is an invitation to JOIN a conversation in progress.

At first, *koanmethod.com* will be your go-to location to dig deeper into the readings list. You'll find links to books, articles, and videos that, over time will be augmented with commentary and conversation.

We hope you will join us there.

Reading List
(Works Cited)

This book would not have been possible without the work of the artists, creators, and scholars whose work is catalogued below. I hope you will visit koanmethod.com to discover more about their work, view videos, and access additional reflections and commentary on the relevance of this work to **the KOAN method.**

1   Estés, Clarissa P. "Do Not Lose Heart, We Were Made for These Times." Creative Commons, 2001, 2016. http://moonmagazine.org/clarissa-pinkola-estes-do-not-lose-heart-we-were-made-for-these-times-2016-12-31/

2   Simpson, Jennifer L. "The Making of Multivocal Culture: (Re)Constructing Community on a University Campus." PhD diss, The University of Colorado at Boulder, 2001.

3   Anzaldua, Gloria. "To Live in the Borderlands." Powerpoetry.org, 1987. https://powerpoetry.org/content/live-borderlands

4   This bibliography contains references from authors representing dozens of cultures, nationalities, and traditions and literature drawn from disciplines as varied as Communication, Psychology, Sociology, Business and Leadership Studies, Neuroscience, Biology, Learning/Education, Ethnic Studies, Women's and Gender Studies, History, Drama/Storytelling, Comparative Religion and Spirituality, Computer Science, Philosophy/Ethics, Legal/Justice Studies, Medicine/Trauma/Healing, Physics, Human Centered Design, Human Development, Performance Training, Natural Systems/Ecology, Social Justice Education Theory and probably a few that I have forgotten to list.

5   Litan, Robert E. "The 'Globalization' Challenge: The U.S. Role in Shaping World Trade and Investment." The Brookings Institution, 2000. https://www.brookings.edu/articles/the-globalization-challenge-the-u-s-role-in-shaping-world-trade-and-investment/

6   Bensman, Todd, and Brian Griffith. "Immigration Brief: Migrant Caravans — America's Next Mass Migration Crisis." Center for Immigration Studies, 2020. https://cis.org/Immigration-Brief/Migrant-Caravans-Americas-Next-Mass-Migration-Crisis

7   Nirenstein, Fiamma. "The Immigration Crisis in Europe." Jerusalem Center for Public Affairs, 2017. https://jcpa.org/immigration-to-europe/the-immigration-crisis-in-europe/

8   Centola, Damon. "Why Social Media Makes Us More Polarized and How to Fix It." *Scientific American*, October 15, 2020. https://www.scientificamerican.com/article/why-social-media-makes-us-more-polarized-and-how-to-fix-it/

9   Vinnakota, Rajiv. "How Social Media Divides Us." The Aspen Institute, January 24, 2017. https://www.aspeninstitute.org/blog-posts/social-media-divides-us/

10   Minson, Julia A. and Francesca Gino. "Managing a Polarized Workforce. How to Foster Debate and Promote Trust. *Harvard Business Review*, March-April, 2022. https://hbr.org/2022/03/managing-a-polarized-workforce

11   Deetz, Stanley, and Jennifer Simpson. "Critical Organizational Dialogue: Open Formation and the Demand of 'Otherness.'" In *Dialogue: Theorizing Difference in Communication Studies*, edited by Rob Anderson, Leslie Baxter, and K Cissna, 141-158. Thousand Oaks, CA: Sage, 2004.

12   Simpson, Jennifer L. (2008). "The Color-Blind Double Bind: Whiteness and the (Im)Possibility of Dialogue." *Communication Theory* 18 (2008): 139-159.

13   Simpson, Jennifer L. and Stanley Deetz. "(Re)defining Cultural Change in Organizations: Structural Determinants at Play." In Abrapcorp's 15th anniversary Commemorative Book, edited by F. Lima, M. Kunsch and A. Sampaio. Bahia/Brazil: Edufba, 2022.

14   Angelou, Maya, bell hooks, and Melvin McLeod. "'There's No Place to Go But Up' — Bell Hooks and Maya Angelou in Conversation." *Lion's Roar*. January, 1998. https://www.lionsroar.com/theres-no-place-to-go-but-up/

15   Johnson, Barry. *Polarity Management: Identifying and Managing Unsolvable Problems*. Amherst, MA: Human Resource Development Press, 2014.

16   Johnson, Barry. *And! Making a Difference by Leveraging Polarity, Paradox or Dilemma* (Volumes 1 & 2). Amherst, MA: Human Resource Development Press, 2020.

17   Emerson, Brian, and Kelly Lewis. *Navigating Polarities: Using Both/And Thinking to Lead Transformation*. Midlothian, VA: Paradoxical Press, 2019.

18   Brubaker, David, and Everett Brubaker. *When the Center Does Not Hold: Leading in an Age of Polarization*. Minneapolis, MN: Fortress Press, 2019.

19   Steinem, Gloria. "A New Egalitarian Life Style." *New York Times*, August 26, 1971, p. 37.

20   Dweck, Carol. *Mindset: The New Psychology of Success*. New York: Ballantine Books, 2007.

21   Dweck, Carol. "The Power of Believing That You Can Improve." TEDxNorrkoping, 2014. https://www.ted.com/talks/carol_dweck_the_power_of_believing_that_you_can_improve

22   Rumi, Jalal al-Din. From "A Great Wagon" in *The Essential Rumi*. Translated by Coleman Barks. New York: Harper One, 2004.

23   Schein, Edgar, and Peter Schein. *Humble Inquiry, Second Edition: The Gentle Art of Asking Instead of Telling*. Oakland, CA: Berrett-Kohler Publishers, 2021.

24   Simpson, Jennifer L. "Engaging Communication: Politically Responsive Theory in Action." In *Engaging Communication, Transforming Organizations: Scholarship of Engagement in Action*, edited by Jennifer L. Simpson and Pamela Shockley-Zalabak. Cresskill, NJ: Hampton Press, 2005.

25   Simpson, J.L. & Allen, B. J. (2005). Engaging difference matters in the classroom. In Simpson, J.L. & Shockley-Zalabak, P. [Eds.] Engaging communication, transforming organizations: Scholarship of engagement in action. Cresskill, NJ: Hampton Press.

Reading List

26   Wheatley, Margaret. *Turning to One Another: Simple Conversations to Restore Hope to the Future.* Oakland, CA: Berrett-Koehler Publishers, 2009.

27   Birdsong, Mia. *How We Show Up: Reclaiming Family, Friendship, and Community.* New York; Hachette Books, 2020.

28   Brown, Brené. *Daring Greatly: How the Courage to Be Vulnerable Transforms the Way We Live, Love, Parent, and Lead.* New York: Avery, 2015.

29   Brown, Brené. *Braving the Wilderness: The Quest for True Belonging and the Courage to Stand Alone.* New York: Random House, 2017.

30   Brown, Brené. *Atlas of the Heart: Mapping Meaningful Connection and the Language of Human Experience.* New York: Random House, 2022.

31   Milton, John P. *Sky Above, Earth Below: Spiritual Practice in Nature.* Boulder, CO: Sentient Publications, 2006..

32   Slaughter, Ann-Marie. (2012). "Why Women Still Can't Have it All." *The Atlantic,* July-August, 2012. https://www.theatlantic.com/magazine/archive/2012/07/why-women-still-cant-have-it-all/309020/

33   Simpson, Jennifer, and E. L. Kirby. "The Invisibility of Identity(s) and Institutions in 'Choices': A White Privilege/Social Class Communicative Response to the 'Opt-Out Revolution.'" *The Electronic Journal of Communication,* 16, 3-4 (2006).

34   Pierrat, Chantal, and Jennifer Simpson. "Leveraging the Power of We." *Emerging Women,* 2019. https://emergingwomen.com/the-power-of-we/

35   Scharmer, C. Otto. *Theory U: Leading from the Future as it Emerges.* San Francisco: Berrett-Koehler, 2007.

36   Simpson, Jennifer L. (2021). "Amplify Your Impact: Making the Most of Mission-Driven Leadership." In *Mission Matters: Business Leaders Edition,* Vol. 5. Beverly Hills, CA: Mission Matters Media, 2021.

37   Saint-Exupéry, Antoine. *The Little Prince.* Translated by R. Howard. Buena Vista, VA: Mariner Press, 2000.

38   Carnegie, Dale. *How to Win Friends and Influence People.* New York: Pocket Books, 1988.

39   Percy, Sally. "What's So Great About Pay Transparency?" *Forbes,* December 2, 2022. https://www.forbes.com/sites/sallypercy/2022/12/02/whats-so-great-about-pay-transparency/?sh=54a17c9e35ce

40   Embrace Global. https://www.embraceglobal.org/

41   Chen, Jane. "A Warm Embrace That Saves Lives." TEDIndia, 2009. https://www.ted.com/talks/jane_chen_a_warm_embrace_that_saves_lives

42   Little Lotus. https://littlelotusbaby.com/

43   Tom's Shoes One for One model. https://www.toms.com/us/about-toms.html

44   Coralus (formerly SheEO). https://coralus.world/about-coralus/

45   IDEO U. Design Thinking Defined. https://designthinking.ideo.com/

46   Chen, Jane. "How I Surfed the Wave that Nearly Drowned My Startup." Hanging Zen, 2016. https://hangingzen.wordpress.com/2016/08/02/how-i-surfed-the-wave-that-nearly-drowned-my-startup/

47   Obama, Michelle. *The Light We Carry*. New York: Crown, 2022..

48   Eisenstein, Charles. *The More Beautiful World Our Hearts Know Is Possible*. Berkeley, CA: North Atlantic Books, 2013..

49   Weil, Simone. "Reflections on War." *Politics*. February, 1945. First published in French in 1933 in "La Critique Sociale." https://libcom.org/article/reflections-war-simone-weil

50   Ryan, Richard, and Edward Deci. Self-Determination Theory: Basic Psychological Needs in Motivation, Development, and Wellness. New York: The Guilford Press, 2018.

51   Pink, Daniel. Drive: The Surprising Truth About What Motivates Us. New York: Riverhead Books, 2011.

52   Heath, Chip, and Dan Heath. *Switch: How to Change Things When Change Is Hard*. New York: Random House, 2010.

53   Duckworth, Angela. *Grit: The Power of Passion and Perseverance*. New York: Scribner, 2018.

54   Goldsmith, Marshall, and Mark Reiter. Triggers: Creating Behavior That Lasts - Becoming the Person You Want to Be. New York: Random House, 2015.

55   Sieden, L. Steven. A Fuller View: Buckminster Fuller's Vision of Hope and Abundance for All. Studio City, CA: Divine Arts Media, 2011.

56   Taylor, Frederick W. The Principles of Scientific Management. Mineola, NY: Dover Publications, 1997.

57   Turkle, Sherry. (2022). "Empathy Rules." *Harvard Business Review*, February 17, 2022. https://hbr.org/2022/02/empathy-rules

58   Zaki, Jamil. (2019). "Making Empathy Central to Your Company Culture." *Harvard Business Review*, May 30, 2019. https://hbr.org/2019/05/making-empathy-central-to-your-company-culture

59   VanDerKolk, Bessel. (2015). *The Body Keeps the Score*. New York: Penguin, 2015.

60   The Conscious Discipline Brain State Model. Conscious Discipline. https://consciousdiscipline.com/methodology/brain-state-model/

61   Lutgen-Sandvik, Pamela, Sarah Tracy, and Jess Alberts. "Burned by Bullying in the American Workplace: Prevalence, Perception, Degree and Impact." *Journal of Management Studies* 44(6):837-862 (2007).

62   Lutgen-Sandvik, Pamela, and Sarah Tracy. "Answering five key questions about workplace bullying: How Communication Scholarship Provides Thought Leadership for Transforming Abuse at Work." *Management Communication Quarterly* 26(1), 3-47 (2012).

63   Schneider, Michael. (2017). "Google Spent 2 Years Studying 180 Teams. The Most Successful Ones Shared These 5 Traits." *Inc. Magazine*, July 19, 2017. https://www.inc.com/michael-schneider/google-thought-they-knew-how-to-create-the-perfect.html

64   Hari, Johann. "Everything You Think You Know About Addiction Is Wrong." TEDGlobal London, 2015. https://www.ted.com/talks/johann_hari_everything_you_think_you_know_about_addiction_is_wrong.

65   Murphy, David, Stephen Joseph, and Pegah Karimi-Mofrad. "Unconditional Positive Self-Regard, Intrinsic Aspirations, and Authenticity: Pathways to

Psychological Well-Being." *Journal of Humanistic Psychology* 60(2) (2017). https://doi.org/10.1177/0022167816688314

66   Wiseman, Liz. Multipliers: How the Best Leaders Make Everyone Smarter. New York: Harper Collins, 2010.

67   Graeber, David, and David Wengrow. *The Dawn of Everything: A New History of Humanity*. Farrar, Strauss, and Giroux, 2021.

68   Rogers, Kristie. (2018). "Do Your Employees Feel Respected?" *Harvard Business Review*, July-August, 2018. https://hbr.org/2018/07/do-your-employees-feel-respected

69   Office of Federal Contract Compliance Programs. "Earnings Disparities." US Department of Labor. https://www.dol.gov/agencies/ofccp/about/data/earnings

70   McQuarry, Kylie. "The Average Salary of Essential Workers in 2020." Business.org, May, 11, 2020. https://www.business.org/finance/accounting/average-salary-of-essential-workers/

71   Bittner, Ashley, and Brigette Lau. (2021). "Women-Led Startups Received Just 2.3% of VC Funding in 2020." *Harvard Business Review*, February 25, 2021. https://hbr.org/2021/02/women-led-startups-received-just-2-3-of-vc-funding-in-2020

72   Saunders, Vicki, and M.J. Ryan. (2014). Think Like A SheEO: Succeeding in the Age of Creators, Makers, and Entrepreneurs. Toronto, Ontario: SheEO Press, 2014.

73   Coralus. About US. https://coralus.world/about-coralus/

74   Coralus World. "2021 SheEO Venture Impact Report." Coralus World, April 22, 2022. https://coralus.world/venture-impact-report-2021/

75   United Nations Department of Economic and Social Affairs. "The 17 Sustainable Development Goals." United Nations Department of Economic and Social Affairs. https://sdgs.un.org/goals

76   History.com Editors. "Nelson Mandela." History. March 29, 2023. https://www.history.com/topics/africa/nelson-mandela

77   Marshall, T.F. "Restorative Justice: An Overview." US Department of Justice: Office of Justice Programs. 1998. https://www.ojp.gov/ncjrs/virtual-library/abstracts/restorative-justice-overview

78   Mingus, Mia. "Transformative Justice: A Brief Description." Transform Harm. January 11, 2019. https://transformharm.org/tj_resource/transformative-justice-a-brief-description/

79   Sivers, Derek. "First Follower: Leadership Lessons From Dancing Guy." Youtube video. 2010. https://www.youtube.com/watch?v=fW8amMCVAJQ

80   Buell, Ryan W. "Operational Transparency: Make Your Processes Visible to Customers and Your Customers Visible to Employees." *Harvard Business Review* (March-April, 2019). https://hbr.org/2019/03/operational-transparency

81   Bernstein, Ethan. "The Transparency Trap". *Harvard Business Review* (October 2014). https://hbr.org/2014/10/the-transparency-trap

82   Scott, Kim. Radical Candor: Kick Ass at Work Without Losing Your Humanity. New York: St. Martin's Press, 2019.

83   Brown, Brené. Dare to Lead: Brave Work. Tough Conversations. Whole Hearts. New York: Random House. New York, 2018.

the KOAN method

84 Covey, Stephen. The Speed of Trust: The One Thing That Changes Everything. New York: Simon & Schuster, 2006.

85 IBM. "What is Open-Source Software?" IBM. https://www.ibm.com/topics/open-source

86 United Nations Education, Scientific, and Cultural Organization. "What is Open Access?" United Nations Education, Scientific, and Cultural Organization (UNESCO). https://en.unesco.org/open-access/what-open-access

87 Schuster, John, Jill Carpenter, and Patricia Kane.. & Carpenter, J.P. The Power of Open-Book Management: Releasing the True Potential of People's Minds, Hearts, and Hands. Hoboken, NJ: Wiley, 1996.

88 The Open University. https://www.open.ac.uk/

89 Smith, Stacy Vanek. (2022). "The Big Reveal: New Laws Require Companies to Disclose Pay Ranges on Job Postings." National Public Radio. November 5, 2022. https://www.npr.org/2022/11/05/1134193927/salary-transparency-range-new-york-pay-laws

90 "Designing the Levi's Commuter Trucker Jacket with Jacquard by Google." IDEO. 2017. https://www.ideo.com/case-study/designing-the-levis-commuter-trucker-jacket-with-jacquard-by-google

91 "A Future Where Food is Never Wasted." Open IDEO. 2016. https://www.openideo.com/case-studies/future-where-food-is-never-wasted

92 Open IDEO Platform. https://www.openideo.com/

93 "Immunization Innovation Lab. An Accelerator to Support Local Innovators in East Africa, Empowering Caregivers and Communities in Public Health." Open IDEO. 2019. https://www.openideo.com/immunization-innovation-lab

94 "Open Educational Resources Support Equity and Flexibility." OER Commons. https://www.oercommons.org/about/

95 "Report of the Presidential Commission on the Space Shuttle Challenger Accident (commonly called the Rogers Commission Report), June 1986 and Implementations of the Recommendations, June 1987." NASA History Office. https://history.nasa.gov/rogersrep/51lcover.htm

96 Sequence of Events—Chernobyl Accident Appendix 1." World Nuclear Association. Updated June, 2019. https://world-nuclear.org/information-library/safety-and-security/safety-of-plants/appendices/chernobyl-accident-appendix-1-sequence-of-events.aspx

97 Dwyer, Jim, and Kevin Flynn. (2002). "FATAL CONFUSION: A Troubled Emergency Response; 9/11 Exposed Deadly Flaws In Rescue Plan." *The New York Times*, June 7, 2002. https://www.nytimes.com/2002/07/07/nyregion/fatal-confusion-troubled-emergency-response-9-11-exposed-deadly-flaws-rescue.html

98 Townsend, Frances F. "The Federal Response to Hurricane Katrina: Lessons Learned." February 2006. http://www.disastersrus.org/katrina/WhiteHouse Katrina report.pdf

99 Holliday, Bertha. "Psychological Perspectives Hurricane Katrina: A Multicultural Disaster." American Psychological Association. May 1, 2016. https://silo.tips/queue/special-section-psychological-perspectives-hurricane-katrina-a-multicultural-dis?&queue_id=-1&v=1683235300&u=NzQuODEuMjE5LjIxMw==

Reading List

100   United States Congress House Committee On Natural Resources. (2011) "Final report of the President's National Commission on the BP Deepwater Horizon Oil Spill and Offshore Drilling: Oversight Hearing Before the Committee on Natural Resources, U.S. House of Representatives, One Hundred Twelfth Congress, first session, Wednesday. Washington: U.S. G.P.O. Retrieved from the Library of Congress, https://lccn.loc.gov/2011388947.

101   Sinek, Simon. Start with Why: How Great Leaders Inspire Everyone to Take Action. New York: Portfolio, 2009.

102   Lorde, Audre. "The Master's Tools Will Never Dismantle the Master's House." In Sister Outsider: Essays and Speeches by Audre Lorde, Berkeley, CA: Crossing Press, 1984.

103   Martin, Roger. "Strategy is Iterative Prototyping." *Harvard Business Review*, June 6, 2014. https://hbr.org/2014/06/strategy-is-iterative-prototyping

104   Senge, Peter. The Fifth Discipline: The Art & Practice of The Learning Organization. New York: Currency, 2006.

105   Tolle, Eckhart. *The Power of Now: A Guide to Spiritual Enlightenment*. Novato, CA: New World Library, 2000.

106   Pema Chödrön Foundation. https://pemachodronfoundation.org/

107   Editors at Chopra.com. "How Breathwork Benefits the Mind, Body, and Spirit." Chopra.com, October 5, 2020. https://chopra.com/articles/how-breathwork-benefits-the-mind-body-and-spirit

108   Vozza, Stephanie. "These Navy SEAL Tricks Will Help You Perform Better Under Pressure." Fast Company, 2019. https://www.fastcompany.com/90354456/these-navy-seal-tricks-will-help-you-perform-better-under-pressure

109   McCraty, R. "Science of the Heart, Volume 2: Exploring the Role of the Heart in Human Performance." HeartMath Institute, 2015. https://www.heartmath.org/research/science-of-the-heart/heart-brain-communication/

110   Senge, Peter, C. Otto Scharmer, Joseph Jaworski, and Betty Sue Flowers. *Presence: Human Purpose and the Field of the Future*. New York: Currency, 2015.

111   Jackson, Phil, and Hugh Delehanty. *Eleven Rings: The Soul of Success*. New York: Penguin, 2013.

112   "Phil Jackson: Zen Master Timeline." ESPN.com (September 7, 2007). https://www.espn.com/nba/news/story?page=PhilJackson-Timeline

113   Jackson, Phil, and Hugh Delehanty. *Sacred Hoops: Spiritual Lessons of a Hardwood Warrior*. New York: Hachette Books, 2012.

114   *The Last Dance*, Episode 10. Film. Directed by Jason Hehir. https://www.imdb.com/title/tt8420184/

115   Dethmer, Jim, Diana Chapman, and Kaley Klemp. The 15 Commitments of Conscious Leadership: A New Paradigm for Sustainable Success. Dethmer, Chapman & Klemp, 2015.

116   Unilever Innovation Challenges. https://www.unilever.com/brands/innovation/innovate-with-us/

117   "Strong full-Year Results Demonstrate Unilever's Resilience and Agility." Unilever.com, February 4, 2021. https://www.unilever.com/news/press-and-media/press-releases/2021/strong-full-year-results-demonstrate-unilevers-resilience-and-agility/

118 Briggs, Bill. "Essential IT: How Unilever Embraced Risk to Cultivate a Remote Workforce – and Cleaner Hands." Unilever.com, February 11, 2021. https://news.microsoft.com/source/features/digital-transformation/essential-it-how-unilever-embraced-risk-to-cultivate-a-remote-workforce-and-cleaner-hands

119 "How Our Hand Sanitiser Business Adapted to Meet Global Demand." Unilever.com, June 12, 2020. https://www.unilever.com/news/news-search/2020/how-our-hand-sanitiser-business-adapted-to-meet-global-demand/

120 Wingard, Jason. (2020). "Don't Fail Fast — Fail Smart." Forbes.com. February 21, 2020. https://www.forbes.com/sites/jasonwingard/2020/02/21/dont-fail-fast--fail-smart/?sh=6743cd3b1b3a

121 Kotter, John. "Hierarchy and Network: Two Structures, One Organization." Harvard Business Review, May 23, 2011. https://hbr.org/2011/05/two-structures-one-organizatio

122 Norwood, Candice. (2021). "How Infrastructure Has Historically Promoted Inequality." *PBS Newshour*, April 23, 2021. Public Broadcasting System. https://www.pbs.org/newshour/politics/how-infrastructure-has-historically-promoted-inequality

123 Brelsford, Christa. "Study Measuring Infrastructure Inequity Addresses Disparities in Growing Cities." Oak Ridge National Laboratory. April 8, 2022. https://www.ornl.gov/news/study-measuring-infrastructure-inequity-addresses-disparities-growing-cities

124 Empire State Development. "Creating Unparalleled Opportunities in Central NY for Generations to Come." https://esd.ny.gov/micron-community-investment-commitments

125 Tampone, Kevin. "Why Micron Picked CNY: Good Schools, a Diverse Workforce and, Yes, Incentives." Syracuse.com. October 4, 2022. https://www.syracuse.com/news/2022/10/why-micron-picked-cny-good-schools-a-diverse-workforce-and-yes-incentives.html

126 West, Cornell. "Justice is What Love Looks Like in Public." Speech given at Howard University, 2011. https://www.youtube.com/watch?v=nGqP7S_WO6o&t=21s

127 Kendall, Mikki. Hood Feminism: Notes from the Women That a Movement Forgot. New York: Penguin, 2021.

128 McGhee, Heather. The Sum of Us: What Racism Costs Everyone and How We Can Prosper Together. New York: One World, 2021.

129 Buck, Pearl. S. A Bridge for Passing: A Meditation on Love, Loss, and Faith. New York: John Day, Co., 1962

130 Rideau, Adam. (2017). "A Solution for Homelessness: Community-Based Problem Solving." TEDxTemecula. https://www.youtube.com/watch?v=KBWflF2jo1k&t=5s

131 Moiz, Mahwish. "Cities That Have Solved Homelessness." CAUF Society. December 15, 2022. https://caufsociety.com/cities-solving-homelessness/

132 US Department of Veterans Affairs. VA National Center on Homelessness Among Veterans: Research-driven Solutions to Prevent and End Homelessness. Housing First Overview. https://www.va.gov/homeless/nchav/models/housing-first.asp

133 Godin, Seth. "In it together." Seth's Blog. October 9, 2021. https://seths.blog/2021/10/in-it-together/

Reading List

134   Godin, Seth. et al. *The Carbon Almanac: It's Not Too Late.* New York: Penguin Random House, 2022. https://thecarbonalmanac.org/

135   Announcing the Winners of the 2022 Data Literacy Awards! https://dataliteracy.com/announcing-the-winners-of-the-2022-data-literacy-awards/

136   Osgood, Dianne, and Mary Elizabeth Sheehan. "Lessons from a Project with No Managers, No Boss, and Everyone Is a Leader." Fast Company. December 14, 2022. https://www.fastcompany.com/90822301/lessons-from-a-project-with-no-managers-no-boss-and-everyone-is-a-leader

137   Ashoka US. "What Ashoka Does." Ashoka.org. 2022. https://www.ashoka.org/en-us

138   Naskar, Abhijit. "Sonnet 9." In Giants in Jeans: 100 Sonnets of United Earth. Amazon: 2021.

139   Fitzsimmons, Grainne, Aaron Kay, and Jae Yun Kim. "'Lean In' Messages and the Illusion of Control." Harvard Business Review. July 30, 1028. https://hbr.org/2018/07/lean-in-messages-and-the-illusion-of-control

140   Robertson, Brian J. Holacracy: The New Management System for a Rapidly Changing World. New York: Henry Holt, 2015.

141   Cumps, Jef. Sociocracy 3.0 – The Novel: Unleash the Full Potential of People and Organizations. Tielt, Belgium: Lannoo Publishers, 2020.

142   Stassyns, Gerrit. (2018). Minsmere Murmuration 17 February 2018. Video. https://www.youtube.com/watch?v=KnndQgIUraQ

143   Van Stijn, Roald. Dutch Starling Murmuration. Utrecht Video. 2019. https://www.youtube.com/watch?v=YjDYE5CUb7Q

144   Brichs, Xavier. (2017). Natura màgica, natura hipnòtica. Video. https://www.youtube.com/watch?v=ID-0D56x30k

145   Meg. Feminist Icons. The Film Artist. https://www.etsy.com/shop/TheFilmArtist?ref=simple-shop-header-name&listing_id=584162157&section_id=20022640

146   Burrage, Darrie Matthew. Reimagining Professionalism. Integrated Work. 2021. https://integratedwork.com/jedi/reimagining-professionalism/

147   Feloni, Richard. "The Way We Do Business Runs Counter to Human Nature and there's Only One Way Forward." Business Insider. December 18, 2018. https://www.businessinsider.com/b-corporation-b-lab-movement-and1-cofounder-2018-11

148   Chouinard, Yvon. "Earth Is Now Our Only Shareholder." Patagonia.com. https://www.patagonia.com/ownership/

149   Remen, Rachel. N. Kitchen Table Wisdom: Stories that Heal. 10th Anniversary Edition. New York: Riverhead Books, 2006.

www.ingramcontent.com/pod-product-compliance
Lightning Source LLC
Chambersburg PA
CBHW061252230426
43665CB00026B/2910